MADE THIS WAY

How to Prepare Kids to Face Today's Tough Moral Issues

LEILA MILLER
with
TRENT HORN

MADE THIS WAY

How to Prepare Kids to
Face Today's Tough Moral Issues

Catholic
Answers
Press

Published by Catholic Answers, Inc.
2020 Gillespie Way
El Cajon, California 92020
1-888-291-8000 orders
619-387-0042 fax
catholic.com

Printed in the United States of America

Cover design by ebooklaunch.com
Interior design by Russell Graphic Design

978-1-68357-097-4
978-1-68357-098-1 Kindle
978-1-68357-099-8 ePub

To St. Monica

Contents

The Reason for This Book

Sometimes it seems like we are living in a bizarre parallel universe. Right is wrong, up is down, men are women (and vice versa). Some Catholic parents don't even realize that our culture has distorted their moral compass, while others recognize the culture's errors but don't know how to explain them to their children.

And that's where the idea for this book began.

One of us is a father of two small boys, has researched these moral issues for over a decade, engages callers about them on live radio, and works full time helping to explain Catholic teachings to them.

The other of us is a mother of eight children and grandmother of several. She has been putting natural-law principles into practice for nearly three decades to teach her children and grandchildren the Church's great wisdom on moral issues. In recent years, she has been mentoring and reassuring anxious Catholic parents as well.

Together we agreed that the best way to equip parents (and others who care about the formation of Catholic children) would be to write a book that teaches truth through *learned experience.* Our book would combine Trent's experience in researching and debating these issues with Leila's experience as a parent and Catholic blogger.

In the pages to follow, we present an overview of child development and a brief explanation of how to use *natural law* in order to understand moral issues. Then we tackle ten of the toughest moral issues of our day, specifically those that touch on the use and misuse of human sexuality.

Each of these ten moral issues has a chapter with three sections dedicated to it. First, a section explaining what the Catholic Church teaches on that particular topic. Then, a section on how to speak to *pre-pubescent* children about this topic. Finally, a section on how to speak to *teens* about this topic.

These chapters are in no way exhaustive; in fact, we had to leave a lot of good stuff on the cutting-room floor. After all, these tough moral issues are important and complex. However, the principles underlying them are simple, and this book will give you the practical tools you need to understand the principles and issues themselves, and then how to teach them to your children. Even if your children are grown adults, or if you interact with children as an aunt, uncle, grandparent, friend, or youth minister, we believe these techniques will vastly improve your conversations.

We also decided that, in order to keep these explanations practical and easy to follow, the book would be written from Leila's point of view as a Catholic parent while also including Trent's research and insights in its explanations and arguments.

Finally, remember that our Lord has given us a holy Church that provides us with grace, truth, and wisdom. We believe that when you are equipped with the right understanding and words, your children will also be equipped to believe, live, and keep the Faith, even in these morally chaotic times.

1

GETTING KIDS
TO HEAVEN

There's an old joke that fits me well:

Before I got married, I had eight theories about raising kids; now I have eight kids and no theories.

When I enrolled my first child in a wonderful Catholic elementary school many years ago, I marveled at all the large families I encountered. I remember seeing a mother of eight come onto campus one day with all her little ones in tow. Her youngest, a two-year-old, was barefoot and had peanut butter crusted around his mouth. As a young mom, I smugly thought that no matter how many children I had, *I* would never allow such a thing.

Now I roll with laughter as I think about all the times my own eight children went out barefoot and with dirty faces!

I share this because I understand that being a parent is hard work, and I don't have any complicated or magical parenting theories to offer. What I do have is the guidance of Christ, his Church, and the witness of the saints, plus the next-best teachers—humility and experience. I respect that parents know their own children better than anyone else does, and so I simply want to give parents, or anyone who interacts with young people (like aunts, uncles, grandparents, and even youth ministers) some tools that have helped me in my own vocation as a Catholic mother hoping to raise saints.

Friend, Parent, or Friendly Parent?

When raising children, there are two extremes we need to avoid: that of *permissive* parents who ditch rules in order to be their child's "friend," and that of *authoritarian* parents who crush their children under harsh rules. (Ironically, these different parenting styles often lead to the same kind of child: one who has low self-esteem and makes bad life choices.)

A better approach is to be an *authoritative* parent.

Unlike permissive parents (who seem to operate from fear or neglectfulness), we aren't merely our child's "friend," and we lay down the law when necessary. We know, as the Bible says, that "all discipline seems painful rather than pleasant; [but] later it yields the peaceful fruit of righteousness to those who have been trained by it" (Heb. 12:11). But unlike authoritarian parents (who seem to operate from anger or pride), we don't teach our children to disdain us or be afraid of us through cold, harsh punishment. We follow St. Paul's instruction to "not provoke your children to anger, but bring them up in the discipline and instruction of the Lord" (Eph. 6:4).

One study of college students showed that whereas children with permissive or authoritarian parents sought advice from their peers, children with authoritative parents were more likely to seek advice from Mom and Dad.[1] This reminds me of a time I had lunch with my friend's lovely teenage daughter who said she went straight to her open-hearted mother when she wanted to know the meaning of a sexual term she'd heard. Her mother gave her a clear answer, placed in the context of Church teaching, and the young woman was satisfied.

"My mom always tells me the truth," she told me, "and I would never think to go to my classmates or friends with that kind of question."

That is exactly what we want our children to say about us, and being a parent who is properly authoritative gets us to that point. My children have always come to me with difficult moral questions precisely because they know that I will not shame them, or give them evasive "non-answers," or tacitly approve immorality. However, the answers I give will always be tailored to their *level of development*.

EDUCATION OR INDOCTRINATION?

Permissive parents may believe it is wrong to "indoctrinate" their children. They may say that a child should be free to make up his own mind on various moral issues. But the word *indoctrinate* literally means "to teach," and even permissive parents indoctrinate their children to value tolerance, open-mindedness, and compassion toward others. So, the question is not, "Will you indoctrinate your children?" but, "With what ideas will you indoctrinate them?"

Made to Receive

Anyone who teaches a child should heed this wisdom from St. Thomas Aquinas: "That which is received is received according to the mode of the receiver."[2]

If you pour water into a glass, it forms a column of water. If you pour water onto a plate, it forms a puddle. You can't get a column of water on a plate because the plate isn't made to receive water in that way. The same is true when it comes to "pouring" knowledge and truth into a child's mind.

A child's brain can only receive what it was made to receive, and children's brains change a lot as they develop. The littlest kids (toddlers and preschoolers) understand right and wrong as a matter of avoiding punishment or receiving rewards. As they get older (elementary school), they understand moral concepts like "fairness" or "justice" (consider how they protest an "unfair" rule).

During this "age of innocence" before puberty (also called the "latency period"), a child's mind is not made to receive graphic or explicit truths about the tough moral issues, especially regarding sexuality. That's why the Pontifical Council on the Family's document *The Truth and Meaning of Human Sexuality* (TMHS) says of pre-adolescents:

> This period of tranquility and serenity must never be disturbed by unnecessary information about sex. During those years, before any physical sexual development is evident, it is normal for the child's interests to turn to other aspects of life....So as not to disturb this important natural phase of growth, parents will recognize that prudent formation in chaste love during this period should be indirect, in preparation for puberty, when direct information will be necessary (78).

Throughout the rest of this book, we will show you how to explain these subjects to little ones if they stumble across them. We'll also show you how to sit down with "big kids" (usually those who have hit puberty) who are ready to hear about these subjects from you. "Without showing anxiety, fear or obsessive concern," *The Truth and Meaning of Human Sexuality* reminds us, "parents will not let cowardice or convenience hinder their work" of educating their children. Instead:

In a *positive and prudent* way, parents will carry out what the Fathers of the Second Vatican Council requested: "It is important to give suitable and timely instruction to young people, above all in the heart of their own families, about the dignity of married love, its role and its exercise; in this way they will be able to engage in honorable courtship and enter upon marriage of their own" (94).

In answering *children's questions,* parents should offer well-reasoned arguments about the great value of chastity and show the intellectual and human weakness of theories that inspire permissive and hedonistic behavior. They will answer clearly, without giving excessive importance to pathological sexual problems (96).

The Worst Thing in the World

Being an independent adult is not just about being able to hold a job and balance a budget. If your child hasn't developed those skills by adulthood, then he might end up in some lawyer's office filing for bankruptcy—which is bad but isn't the *worst* thing in the world.

What's worse is your child becoming an adult and not knowing the difference between good and evil. Or, if he does know it, not having the maturity and the will to choose what is good. If our children aren't developed in *those* areas, then they might end up separated from God for all eternity—which *is* the worst thing in the world.

So what's holding back so many parents from teaching their children these important truths about right and wrong? Well, some may be embarrassed about their own past (or current) lifestyles and not want to discuss the issues for fear of being considered a hypocrite. Others may not want to have a confrontation with their kids, hoping that if they are just "nice" or passive, then everything will work out. Or, they think they can simply say, "This is what we believe!" or "We don't do that!" because they don't know how to share *the reasonable foundation* for our beliefs.

If there is one underlying truth I have found in forming my own teenagers, it's this: they will accept and embrace a worldview that *makes sense to them*—even if that worldview is difficult to live out in our culture. They are "made to receive" not just rules or Church teaching, but *reasons* that support those teachings. And, praise God, those reasons can be adapted for any child, because they are based on a universal principle called *the natural law*.

2

UNDERSTANDING NATURAL LAW

My teens always looked forward to the homilies of a particular priest, because he made the truths of Catholicism exciting and substantial. He inspired us to *think* about our Faith, and one way he did that was through a simple piece of philosophy. He said, "If we want to know what is real and true, we must always ask, 'What is the nature of a thing?'" Another way to put it would be, "What *is* this thing and what is it made *for*?"

These questions unlock the force of the natural law, guiding us to understand more deeply the truth, goodness, and beauty that is our Catholic faith.

The Nature of Natural Law

The first time I heard the term "natural law" was when my friend Nikolas Nikas of the Bioethics Defense Fund gave a presentation at my parish. By that time I had already spent many years teaching my children, my RCIA students, and others about God's universal moral law and how it can be known by the use of reason alone—but I had never heard it called by the name of *natural law*. Nik demonstrated how America's Constitution and our system of laws were based on natural-law principles that transcend any merely human laws based on popular opinion or human will (what is called *positive law*).

Abraham Lincoln, for example, cited moral truths that could be known through reason when he worked to deliver our nation from the evil of slavery. In a debate with Stephen Douglas, Lincoln said that slavery wasn't just a political issue but one that represented "the eternal struggle between these two principles—right and wrong."[3] A century later, Martin Luther King, Jr. was told that racial segregation was the "law of the land" and must be obeyed. MLK replied that *unjust* laws may be disobeyed. As he sat in jail for disobeying those laws, he wrote:

> How does one determine whether a law is just or unjust? A just law is a man-made code that squares with the moral law or the law of God. An unjust law is a code that is out of harmony with the moral law. To put it in the terms of St. Thomas Aquinas: an unjust law is a human law that is not rooted in eternal law and natural law.[4]

Natural law is another term for the universal moral law of God. Aquinas said that the natural law "is nothing other than the light of understanding infused in us by God, whereby we understand what must be done and what must be avoided."[5] This law is universal because everyone—including people who have never received divine revelation—can know it. St. Paul proclaimed that even people who have never encountered something as basic as the Ten Commandments can still apprehend God's important moral truths, because "what the law requires is written on their hearts" (Rom. 2:15).

Popes have used natural law to appeal to the world's consciences. In recent memory, Pope Pius XII's first encyclical was written to oppose humanity's "drift toward chaos," which he blamed on "the disregard, so common nowadays, and the forgetfulness of the natural law itself" (*Summi Pontificatus* 28). And Paul VI, writing in *Humanae Vitae* on the nature of human sexuality and the evils of contraception, stressed that "this teaching is in harmony with human reason."

Some Catholics today argue against the use of natural law to instruct, calling it outdated or ineffective and suggesting pedagogical techniques that they consider more in line with modern sensibilities. But no less a thinker than Robert Cardinal Sarah has affirmed that "the Church's social teaching argues on the basis of reason and natural law, namely on the basis of what is in accord with the nature of every human being."[6]

It is because of the natural law that Christians, Jews, Muslims, Buddhists, Hindus, and even atheists and agnostics can hear their consciences tell them what they *may* do, what they *must* do, and what they *must never* do.

Natural law explains people's deep-seated understanding that crimes like murder and theft are wrong, whereas charitable acts like feeding the hungry and clothing the naked are right. It helps us instinctively relate such actions to the way human beings have been made. When we ask, "What is human life *for*?" or "What is the *nature* of a human being?" we want to know our ultimate goal in life and how to reach that goal. Natural law shows us both, or as professor Charles Rice says, it's "a set of manufacturer's directions written into our nature so that we can discover through reason how we ought to act."[7]

Just as we would not harm our car's mechanical nature by putting molasses in the tank—which is made for gas—we should not harm our human nature by acting immorally; that is, in ways that contradict its design.

But before discussing natural law any further we need to address some common misunderstandings about it.

What Natural Law is Not

Natural law is not the same as the "laws of nature." Scientific laws explain how matter and energy behave in the physical world. These laws cannot be "disobeyed" because they describe what *usually* happens rather than what *should* happen. For example, the law of gravity (science) describes how a falling bomb accelerates toward the earth. Natural law (morality) tells us whether it is right or wrong to drop the bomb on a certain target.

Natural law is not "what happens with other mammals in nature." When Christians say that certain human behaviors go against nature, they mean that those acts contradict how human beings ought to act, not merely what happens in the natural world. Humans are animals, but we are rational animals, and so we should not make the behavior of lower animals our standard of morality. Lots of behaviors are "natural" for other animals, like stealing, forced sex, or infanticide, but that doesn't make those behaviors natural for rational human beings.

Natural law is not "what feels natural to me." A person may have a strong inclination to eat a whole box of cookies or a persistent desire to cheat on a spouse, but the consequences of those decisions show that we shouldn't always follow our "natural feelings." This doesn't mean we should never follow our instincts and feelings; it just means we should use our minds to tell us which of them we should follow.

C.S. Lewis used the analogy of a piano to explain the relationship between our animal instincts that tempt us to do evil and our rational minds that know the moral law.[8] He said that instincts are like the keys on the piano, and morality (the natural law) is like the sheet music that tells us when to play the keys at the right time. For example, the fight instinct is good for a young boy if a stranger is trying to pull his sister into a car and abduct her; it's bad if he is frustrated with his sister during play and uses fists to settle the matter. Likewise, the flight instinct is good when running away from a tsunami; it's cowardly when running away from an infant drowning in a play pool.

Unlike the lower animals, we human beings are created with an intellect and a will (made in God's image), which means that we are the only ones with the ability to reason morally—to *choose* between right and wrong. According to St. Thomas Aquinas's classic definition, natural law is man's participation in God's eternal law, an intersection between human reason and divine wisdom.[9]

DIFFERENT THEORIES, SAME GOAL

In the academic world, there are different theories about how to apply natural-law principles in defense of traditional morality. However, in order to keep this book accessible to the average parent, I am not going to wade into the finer academic points. Instead, I'm just going to share what we think are the best non-religious arguments that support Catholic morality and credit a variety of philosophers and theologians in the process.

The Benefits of Natural Law

Although natural law originates with God, it is not strictly a religious concept.

Some truths of the Faith can be known only through divine revelation (e.g., the Trinity, the nature of the sacraments), and divine revelation—such as the Ten Commandments—can also more clearly reveal the truths of the natural law. But in a discussion with a non-believer, it would be futile to rely solely on divine revelation. Non-believers don't care one whit about the evidence of Scripture or Church documents, but through discussion of the natural law we can appeal to "what we can't not know," whether one has the gift of faith or not.[10] Each soul is designed by God to be attracted to truth, and we all have brains that can reason. Natural law is the only firm foundation that can ground a debate (try debating based on "feelings" and see how far you get!).

We can also appeal to natural law when secularists accuse Christians of "imposing" morality on them. We can show them that natural law *prevents* the unjust imposition of an unsound morality, because it is a safeguard against tyranny and oppression. The convictions of Nazi war criminals at the Nuremberg Trials were not based on man-made law (everything they did was perfectly legal in Germany), but rather on a universal morality that was recognizable by the world community.

The greatest benefit of natural law is that it is not arbitrary. Some people think that Catholics blindly follow whatever the Bible or the pope says, but our faith does not consist of such commands. The *Catechism* says, "God's almighty power is in no way arbitrary: 'In God, power, essence, will, intellect, wisdom, and justice are all identical. Nothing therefore can be in God's power which could not be in his just will or his wise intellect'" (271).

God loves us, so not only his positive commandments but also the moral laws we discover through reason will always correspond to what is good for us as human beings; they will never just be a set of nonsensical, disconnected, inconsistent, incoherent rules.

If anything, it is *our culture that is arbitrary*, because it reduces morality to mere popular opinion or the will of the powerful ("might makes right"). Children who are raised in this culture of moral relativism, especially those who lack the stability of an intact family, can quickly become disoriented and lost. Yet, if we can provide them a moral foundation through the natural law—if we can help them see that the way they should act corresponds to the way they are made—they will feel safe and secure in the truth, even as the rest of the world stumbles in darkness. Children who understand God's created order and how "everything fits together" are more likely to become holy, healthy, and happy adults, leading others to Christ and eternal glory as well.

REMEMBER...

- The natural law is simply the universal moral law, accessible to all people by the light of human reason.

- Natural law is not the same as the "laws of nature" like gravity, nor is it simply "what happens in nature" or "what feels natural to me." It is the law of God revealed in our very humanity, written in our consciences.

- Natural law is not an arbitrary set of rules. Instead, it is like an "instruction manual" that tells us how to live according to the design of our human nature, providing our lives with meaning, peace, and joy.

3

SEX OUTSIDE OF MARRIAGE

What the Church Teaches

Even with Madonna's "Like a Virgin" playing on the radio and widespread sexual activity among my peers, when I attended public high school in the 1980s most of us still believed in the "ideal" of saving sex for marriage—even if we didn't live up to it. Today, however, even the memory of that ideal has all but faded from our culture.

In 1972, only a quarter of adults believed sex before marriage was "not wrong at all," but forty years later that figure had jumped to more than half.[11] Thirty years ago, less than half of high school seniors supported cohabiting before marriage, but today, two-thirds of them agree with this statement: "It is usually a good idea for a couple to live together before getting married in order to find out whether they really get along."[12]

One thing that hasn't changed, however, is the heart's desire for perfect happiness, something casual sex can never provide. Those who care about "sexual health" would be edified to learn and understand the Church's teachings on marriage and sexuality.

Let's Think About Sex, Baby

Each of the moral confusions we discuss in this book stems from a failure to understand the nature of sex and the meaning of marriage. But none of us can fully appreciate the "badness" of sex outside marriage until we understand the goodness of sex within marriage. Our culture does a lot of talking about sex, but I propose that we all need to *think* about what sex means. What Catholic author Frank Sheed wrote in 1953 is just as true today:

> The typical modern man practically never thinks about sex. He dreams of it, of course, by day and by night; he craves for it; he pictures it, is stimulated or depressed by it, drools over it. But this frothing, steaming activity is not thinking. Drooling is not thinking, picturing is not thinking, craving is not thinking, dreaming is not thinking. Thinking means bringing the power of the mind to bear: thinking about sex means striving to see sex in its innermost reality and in the function it is meant to serve.[13]

Body and Soul

Let's start with the basics. Human beings are created as a union of physical body and immortal soul. This union sets us apart from the lower animals, whose mortal bodies have mortal souls, both of which perish at death. It also sets us apart from the angels, who are pure (immortal) spirits without bodies.

The soul is the life-giving principle of the body. It's literally what makes a living body different from a dead one. And not only do our immortal human souls survive the death of our bodies, they are also *rational,* enabling us to exercise moral reason instead of relying on instinct alone (as lower animals, with their *sensitive* souls, do).

But although our souls distinguish us from lower animals, human beings are not merely souls trapped in bodies, as if we were "ghosts in machines" that seek to escape the body at death. We are not angels and can never be. Instead, human beings are *embodied persons*. This means we don't just *have* bodies, we *are* bodies—and although death temporarily separates us from our body, at the resurrection of the dead we will be restored to a bodily existence for all eternity! All of this means that our bodily actions have consequences both in this life and in the next. This is especially true when it comes to sex, because sex is the one bodily act that is ordered toward creating new human beings with immortal souls—a power that even angels do not possess!

Through our embodied existence, specifically through our maleness or femaleness, we express the good of our sexuality. The *Catechism* is clear: "Everyone, man and woman, should acknowledge and accept his sexual identity. Physical, moral, and spiritual difference and complementarity are oriented toward the goods of marriage and the flourishing of family life" (2333).

Marriage showcases the beauty of male/female complementarity, because when a married man and woman become "one flesh" through the marital act (sexual intercourse), their bodies are *ordered toward a good that exists beyond themselves* as individuals. In that single act, husband and wife unite to form a complete, bodily union that is designed to bring a child into existence—a new human person who becomes a permanent sign of their marital love.

Even from a non-religious perspective, the serious and enduring consequences of sex show that it is only appropriate when it is an expression of lifelong love and fidelity—or what we call *marriage*. When sex occurs outside of this context, we can be certain that pain, injustice, and heartbreak (which were never a part of God's plan for sex) will not be far behind.

> ### NOTHING TO BE ASHAMED OF
> Remember that sex is not a shameful or bad thing, and the Church does not teach that it is. In fact, *The Truth and Meaning of Human Sexuality* says that parents should not "give the false impression that sex is something shameful or dirty, because it is a great gift of God who placed the ability to generate life in the human body, thereby sharing his creative power with us" (96).

Don't Deface God's Temple

The *Catechism* says that the mutual love that exists between man and woman "becomes an image of the absolute and unfailing love with which God loves man. It is good, very good, in the Creator's eyes" (1604). The sacrament of matrimony doesn't even become indissoluble until the husband and wife have consummated the marriage, becoming "one flesh" through sexual intercourse. So we can see that, far from demonizing sex, the Church reveres it as an essential part of a sacrament!

If sex is the expression of marital love, it follows that any sexual activity outside of marriage is a fraudulent expression of intimacy. Why? Because sex outside of the marriage bond cannot express the permanent, total gift of self that God intended. An unmarried couple has not made any public, marital vows to which the Church and the couple's community will hold them accountable. This is why the *Catechism* says:

> Fornication is carnal union between an unmarried man and an unmarried woman. It is gravely contrary to the

dignity of persons and of human sexuality which is naturally ordered to the good of spouses and the generation and education of children. Moreover, it is a grave scandal when there is corruption of the young (2353).

Marriage and sex are intrinsically linked, and neither is simply a "private affair" because marriage is the foundation of every human *society*. Consequently, the misuse of sex is a serious matter. In 1 Corinthians 6:9, St. Paul says that neither adulterers nor the "sexually immoral" or "fornicators" will enter the kingdom of heaven.

Adultery is sexual sin involving at least one married person. Fornication, on the other hand, is sexual sin between unmarried people. Paul calls those who engage in fornication *pornoi*, which we recognize from English words like *pornography*.[14] Paul was extremely concerned about the misuse of a gift from God that leads to a distortion of our very selves. In 1 Corinthians 6:16-20 he writes:

> Do you not know that he who joins himself to a prostitute becomes one body with her? For, as it is written, "The two shall become one flesh." But he who is united to the Lord becomes one spirit with him. Shun immorality. Every other sin which a man commits is outside the body; but the immoral man sins against his own body. Do you not know that your body is a temple of the Holy Spirit within you, which you have from God? You are not your own; you were bought with a price. So glorify God in your body.

Mr. and Mrs. Individuality

People often think their bodies are just "their own," and so no one else has the right to tell them what to do with those bodies—especially in the realm of sexuality. Even secular scholars recognize this attitude, as a recent study on teenage sexuality found that "rising cultural individualism has produced an increasing rejection of traditional social rules, including those against non-marital sex."[15]

Our task is to show young people (as well as adults who act like young people) that "traditional social rules" related to sex are not arbitrary killjoys that we can discard at our pleasure and whim. Instead, God's natural law reveals that his plan for our sexuality is written into our very being. When it is followed, this plan leads to a joy-filled life. When it is rejected, we invite misery and despair.

So let's start with how to navigate this topic when our youngest children stumble upon it, then move on to showing teens the sensible reasons they should save sex for marriage.

REMEMBER...

- Human beings are not merely minds or souls that inhabit bodies. Our bodies are an essential part of our identity and what we do with them matters.

- Sex is a very good thing that God created for the expression of lifelong, committed love and the procreation of children from that love.

- Sex outside of the marriage bond constitutes the grave sin of fornication because it misuses the gift of marital love God gave us.

SEX OUTSIDE OF MARRIAGE

Advice for Little Kids

First comes love, then comes marriage, then comes a baby in the baby carriage!

There was a time when that little playground rhyme was known by every child in America; it was a joyful way to learn and understand the correct and expected cultural order of things. In today's culture, however, children are taught that there is no correct order at all. Our task is to restore in children's minds the proper order of marriage, sex, and babies, and we should begin to do that as early as possible.

The Years of Innocence

As we learn in *The Truth and Meaning of Human Sexuality*, ideally a child's first introduction to sex should not be through a discussion of genital activity; instead, it should come indirectly, through the observation that Mommy, an auntie, or one of Mommy's friends is having a new baby (76). This helps children place babies (and implicitly, sex) in the context of marriage. Conversations with little ones about pregnancy might go like this:

> Do you see Mommy's tummy getting bigger? That's your little baby brother or sister inside! This little one is safe and happy, nestled right up to Mommy's heart! Isn't it so beautiful that after Daddy and Mommy got married, God gave us babies to love? That is what makes marriage so special, and now we all can love one another forever, just like we love God and he loves us!

You should teach your littlest ones that only married people should have babies, without giving the explicit details of how babies are made. When a child asks, "Where do babies come from?" you can tell him that babies come from mommies and daddies and that God helps a baby grow inside the mommy. I personally have never encountered a problem using the colloquial "Mommy's tummy" when speaking about an unborn baby's location, but if you're worried that your child will think babies grow in the stomach, you can always use the word *womb* instead (to kids, it sounds like a special kind of "room"), or *uterus* if you use medical terms early.

Occasionally, you'll get a child who is not satisfied with this kind of answer; for me, that was my eldest. Precocious and curious, my daughter came with questions at the tender age of six and kept pushing past the usual answers: "But *how* does God make those babies?" she asked. "How does the baby *get* in the mommy's tummy?"

She was relentless, and so I finally gave her some very basic biology and gently explained "where the parts go" to make a baby. She had little brothers, so she was already familiar with the differing anatomy of male and female. That was more than enough for her, and I am pretty sure she was sorry she asked! I also carefully explained to my daughter that because this was a very holy and private matter, she should not discuss this with any of her peers at her Catholic school.

Adults are obligated to protect every child's innocence, so for a long time after our conversation I worried that I had told her too much too soon. Fortunately, this child, now a wife and mother, remained committed to her faith and to chastity even after her early introduction to reproductive biology. God is merciful, and he honors our sincere efforts to do his will!

None of my other seven children pressed for answers this young, and this speaks to the uniqueness of every child. When your children come to you with questions like this, you must prayerfully determine what information they are ready to receive based on what you know of your child. But however young they are, the overarching message can be taught: when a man and a lady love each other and get married, God helps their special love become the gift of a baby that grows inside of Mommy. Marriage was made by God for this special love between mommies and daddies, and it's within marriage that babies belong.

USING QUESTIONS TO GIVE ANSWERS

If an issue catches you off guard, you can buy time to compose your thoughts by gently asking your child, "Where did you hear that word?" and "What do you think it means?"

The questions will help you gauge what your child knows and determine what answer would be most appropriate. There is no need for a parent to start a discussion about sex only to find out that it

> was not yet necessary! Remember that such ques-
> tioning should not be done in an accusatory tone, as
> if your child were in trouble. You want to create a
> climate in which your child will always be comfort-
> able coming to you with sensitive questions.

When Innocence Is Violated

Childhood should be a carefree time, unburdened by adult
issues like sex. But even the most vigilant parents can't always prevent a violation of their child's innocence. So what
do we do when our little ones hear about sex or its details
from the media, school, or friends?

Here is my basic rule when a child receives too much
sexual information, too soon: *don't freak out!* Remember
the words of Jesus: "Can any of you by worrying add a
single moment to your life-span?" (Matt. 6:27, NABRE).
We can't, so let's replace worry with trust as we work to
counter the effects of a child's premature exposure to sexual information.

Feel confident that God entrusted you with your children,
and know that he is always present to help you love and guide
them through our culture's moral snares. When too-early exposure occurs, "parents will have to begin to give carefully
limited sexual information, usually to correct immoral and
erroneous information or to control obscene language."[16]

So when a little child asks, "What is sex?" or has been
exposed to an explicit description of sex, you can explain
that "any type of acts using our private parts in order to get
pleasure is something God reserves for married grownups,
never for kids or for unmarried people. This is so that everyone can be happy and healthy, including little babies that
come from the love of married people!"

Of course, some children will understandably be confused when they encounter family situations that don't follow God's plan for our sexuality. For example, if a friend's parents are cohabiting, a child might ask, "Why aren't Julie's parents married?" Or, if an unmarried sister or cousin is pregnant, a youngster might say, "But I thought you had to be married to have a baby?" When situations like this come up, you can explain in this way:

> Men and women can make babies, but they are supposed to wait until they are married to make them. Mommies and daddies are supposed to love their babies forever, so before they have babies, they promise to love each other forever by getting married. That's what marriage is for, and God gave us this rule about marriage so we could be happy, and so every child could be raised by his or her own mommy and daddy in a forever family.
>
> Some people don't follow God's rules,* and don't wait to be married to have babies, because they don't know God, or they may not understand why his rules are so important. Let's pray for them so that they can know God better and be able to love each other just like God loves them!

Such an answer should satisfy most every small child, without your having to discuss the details of sexual reproduction. In fact, these answers, with more sophisticated wording, will be helpful throughout most of their elementary

---

* Of course, a woman can become pregnant without having consented to sex. If such a scenario presents itself to your child, you may want to modify this approach at your discretion.

school education and can be supplemented with discussions of biology when appropriate.

Of course, your child's entrance into puberty will require significant changes to your answers and approach. With the onset of puberty, sex will no longer be an issue "out there" but a confusing, powerful desire "in here" that your child will have to work through with your guidance and help. So, let's now discuss how we should talk about premarital sex with the children who are most at risk for engaging in it.

REMEMBER . . .

- We must do our best to protect "the years of innocence" with no explicit sex talk. We place babies in the context of married mommies and daddies. If your child hears about sex too early, explain it in the context of a gift God gives to husbands and wives in marriage.

- Don't freak out if kids stumble on sexual content, but ask them questions to see what they know and help you gather your thoughts.

- God doesn't give a teaching that can't be understood; children have been taught that "sex is for marriage" for millennia, and modern children can understand truth. Be confident!

SEX OUTSIDE OF MARRIAGE

Advice for Big Kids

Once in a conversation on my Facebook page, a commenter stated her view on sex: "There is no universal purpose, beauty, or reason to sex—that is up to individuals to decide for themselves." Trent saw this attitude in a documentary he filmed that asked college students, "What is sex for?" The most popular answer was: "That's up to each person to decide for himself."

This is a common belief of millions who claim that sex isn't *for* anything in particular. Sex can be for pleasure, or recreation, or stress relief, or a cure for boredom. It can be no more significant or meaningful than eating ice cream! It all depends on how you feel about it.

The best way to get past this feelings-based approach to sex is by applying the natural-law principles we learned in chapter two. Remind your teens that they should ask what sex is *made for*, and use the answer to that question to guide their moral decisions.

Designed for Marital Love

If sex is just for pleasure, as millions say, why do so many people become distraught when their "significant other" has sex with someone else? This pain—universally understood and documented in literature, songs, and poems throughout millennia—is a huge hint that sex isn't as casual or meaningless as many claim it is.

Some may say that sex is actually the way we express a deep emotional connection to another person. But we can have a deep emotional connection to many different people (friends, siblings, parents, children) with whom it would be wrong to have a *sexual* connection. So, what distinguishes sexual relationships from all other kinds of human intimacy?

The answer is found in the design of the body.

When we look at the body, including the sexual faculty itself, we see that sex is *ordered toward* a lifelong consequence: the conception of a child. This truth is a signpost indicating that men and women should not engage in sex before they've made the lifelong commitment (marriage) that provides the foundation for the fruit of that act (a baby).

Of course, many people will say that these consequences can be avoided by contraceptive use (which we will address later), rendering sex outside of marriage no big deal. But even if contraception didn't fail often (and boy, it does), premarital sex would still be morally wrong with grave consequences. Why? Because it turns people into liars.[17]

Deceptive Body Language

Your teen will probably agree that, in general, the words we speak should be honest and truthful. But we can also "speak" with our bodies to express ideas. For example, a handshake can mean "pleased to meet you" and a hug can mean "I am here for you." When people use their bodies to communicate what is *not* true, they often experience discomfort.

Think about the uneasiness you feel when you're forced to stand too close to a stranger on a bus or subway. Your bodies are expressing the language of social intimacy because they are so close together, but that intimacy doesn't match the truth of the situation—you don't even know each other! Similarly, sex outside of marriage expresses the intimacy of a permanent one-flesh union, but in a relationship (no matter how long it's been going on) that has no such commitment. It is a lie, told through the body, that speaks louder than words.

Teens can understand this idea. A girl may feel this discomfort when she doesn't want the guy to see her naked. She may want to "get it over with" in hopes that sex will lead to a fulfilling relationship. Or, she may be sexually willing but feel crushed when the boy does not contact her again. Boys, on the other hand, may resist being affectionate after sex or even refuse to talk to the girl they've slept with, because they don't want to express with their hearts the deep, marital love they expressed with their bodies.

This discomfort is not some culturally induced guilt from a bygone era; it's a strong signal that this type of vulnerable intimacy is only appropriate in the *safety* of a lifelong, exclusive commitment. Sex outside of marriage is wrong because the body turns a beautiful truth ("I reveal and give my whole self to you in an irrevocable gift") into a selfish and harmful lie. When your teens ask, "Why is sex before marriage wrong?" you can give them a simple, reasonable answer:

> Sex exists for the expression of marital love. Sex outside of marriage uses the body to express a permanent, fruitful union of love that doesn't exist between

unmarried couples. Sex outside of marriage is a lie, and we must never lie to the people we claim to love.

For Boys

When teaching virtues to boys, you should appeal to their innate desire to be a hero. Give a boy a truly noble task that must be accomplished, and he will naturally rise to the challenge. Even preschool boys use sticks as swords to defeat bad guys and save the maiden in distress. We should cultivate this desire, channeling the power of masculinity toward the good.

Tell your son that the Latin word *virtus*—from which we get *virtue*—means "manliness, bravery, worth, moral excellence." I remind my sons that the most powerful man in the world is the one with the most self-control, and that the man who cannot control his passions is nothing more than a slave to them.

Though many teen boys are conditioned to believe that having sex will prove their manhood, you must help your son understand that sex outside of marriage makes him the villain, not the hero. Through one selfish act, he could destroy a girl's innocence and break her heart into a thousand pieces. At his judgment, what will your son tell God if his "sexual conquest" led to a girl's spiritual destruction?

A true hero defeats the dragon and saves the girl; he doesn't cooperate with the dragon in order to destroy her!

Sexual sin destroys souls, but it also destroys bodies. We must teach our boys that premarital sex may literally endanger someone's life. I can tell you that our pro-life boys are shaken to their core when we remind them, "If you get a girl pregnant, she may abort your child, and you can't stop her. You have no legal rights at all, and you may not even find out about the pregnancy until after your child has been killed. You will have to live with that knowledge for the rest of your life."

Another scenario that boys rarely consider, but that gets their attention: "If you get a girl pregnant and you don't marry her, you will likely have little to no say in how your child is raised. You also will have no control over any other men who will come in and out of your child's life."

Teens understand and appreciate honesty and straight talk. There is no need to dwell excessively on these scenarios, lest they be dismissed as wild scare tactics, but we must tell our sons the bad news about sin even as we encourage them with the good news that God made them to be heroes who protect women and children.

Boys will take up the challenge of true manhood *if supported and encouraged by people they trust and admire*. Because the culture at large no longer encourages the virtue of chastity as it once did, it is up to parents—especially fathers—and the Church community to fulfill that task.

For Girls

Where a boy innately wants to know that he's "got what it takes," a girl innately wants to know that she is cherished, captivating, lovely—and worth fighting for. When teaching your daughter about the virtue of chastity, appeal to her sense of intrinsic worth and to her right not to be used, by anyone, as a mere object of pleasure. Ask her, "What words do you want people to use to describe your future husband?"

Faithful? Courageous? Wise? Honest? Hardworking? Loyal? Patient? Loving? Kind?

These are all examples of virtue, and whether they can articulate it or not, deep down women want a *virtuous* man. I have even debated staunch secular feminists who admitted, though only in private, that they would love for a man to protect, provide, and care for them. A man who uses women sexually does not possess those attributes that a woman desires.

Make clear to your daughters that there is no double standard in your home or in the Church: both women *and* men are expected to be chaste, and she should never have to offer sex in order to "prove her love," or in exchange for the opportunity to make her boyfriend a "better man."

When my own girls were in high school, my cautionary tales were taken seriously because they were playing out all around them: girls who were used sexually (or who used others) were left with broken hearts and crushed spirits, some having to agonize over the consequences of being pregnant without a husband.

So how, exactly, does a young woman attract a virtuous man instead of a user? The answer is: "character attracts character." If a girl wants a virtuous guy to be courageous and ask her out, then she has to practice courage, too. She shouldn't put herself out there sexually just because she fears no one will date a prude, and she needs to be strong enough to hold potential suitors to the highest standards.

This doesn't mean setting the impossible standard of nothing less than a perfect St. Joseph! (I've seen Catholic women do that, unfortunately.) But her task is to call men to be the best they can be. As Archbishop Fulton Sheen said so eloquently:

> To a great extent the level of any civilization is the level of its womanhood. When a man loves a woman, he has to become worthy of her. The higher her virtue, the more noble her character, the more devoted she is to truth, justice, goodness, the more a man has to aspire to be worthy of her. The history of civilization could actually be written in terms of the level of its women.[18]

Virtuous Fire

Chastity is one of the virtues, and virtues are for every human being in every state of life, no exceptions. They are about having the strength to do the right thing at the right time in spite of temptations. So chastity is not about "not having sex" (that's *abstinence*); rather, it is about mastering our sexual desires so that we control them and they don't control us.

It is only by mastering the virtues that we can ever have lasting joy anyway! Veteran moms Kimberly Hahn and Mary Hasson offer an analogy that teens will understand:

> Fire that is properly contained—used for the right purpose and in the right place—gives us warmth and light, beauty and happiness . . . . In contrast, a fire that is ignited and burns without boundaries leaves destruction, pain, and ashes in its wake . . . . God surpasses all expectations when we use sexuality as he wishes.[19]

REMEMBER . . .

- The body speaks a language, and sex is the way human beings express permanent, fruitful (marital) love. This means sex outside of marriage is a lie, and we mustn't be liars.

- Boys should be challenged to practice self-mastery and use their strength to protect women and children.

- Girls should value their self-worth and practice virtues that attract virtuous men.

4

SAME-SEX MARRIAGE
What the Church Teaches

On June 26, 2015, in a 5-4 decision that the American bishops called "profoundly immoral and unjust," the United States Supreme Court decided in *Obergefell v. Hodges* that marriage may no longer be understood as the lifelong conjugal union of a man and woman.[20] The Supreme Court had made grave mistakes against the natural law before, allowing:

- Slavery in *Dred Scott v. Sanford* (1857)
- Racial segregation in *Plessy v. Ferguson* (1896)
- Sterilization of the mentally handicapped in *Buck v. Bell* (1922)
- Killing of unborn children through abortion in *Roe v. Wade* (1973)

The law is not magic. It cannot make black people less human or unborn children un-human; it cannot make women turn into men and it cannot make marriage exist between two men or two women. The state can play with words, but it cannot change reality. That is why the Congregation for the Doctrine of the Faith (CDF) says that, in cases where marriage has been legally redefined to include same-sex couples, "clear and emphatic opposition is a duty. One must refrain from any kind of formal cooperation in the enactment or application of such gravely unjust laws."[21]

But how do we help people see the reality of marriage when it has been clouded by a legal fiction?

The Ends of Marriage

The biggest trap faithful Catholics fall into when discussing "same-sex marriage" (SSM) or "marriage equality" is using the other side's language. We often waste time explaining why we don't believe a same-sex couple should be "allowed" to marry when we should focus on a more fundamental question: *What is marriage?*

If marriage is just something that celebrates "romantic love" between adults (what has been called the "relational" view of marriage*), then there's no reason same-sex couples, or even polygamous "groupings," should not marry. But, if marriage is fundamentally about a man, a woman, and the children that may come from that union (the "conjugal" view of marriage), then SSM is like a square circle—it's a logical impossibility.[22]

No one can be neutral on this question. If you claim to believe in "marriage equality" or "the right to marry" then you have the responsibility to know what marriage *is*. Only in defining our terms can we know if someone is right or wrong in promoting or opposing same-sex marriage.

So, what is marriage? The *Catechism* says:

---

* The majority opinion for the *Obergefell* decision, authored by Anthony Kennedy, claims: "The nature of marriage is that, through its enduring bond, two persons together can find other freedoms, such as expression, intimacy, and spirituality."

The marriage covenant, by which a man and a woman form with each other an intimate communion of life and love, has been founded and endowed with its own special laws by the Creator. By its very nature it is ordered to the good of the couple, as well as to the generation and education of children. Christ the Lord raised marriage between the baptized to the dignity of a sacrament (1660).

Jesus spoke about marriage as a one-flesh union that only husbands and wives can form. He even implied those who could not physically consummate a marriage (by performing the marital act) were not called to the vocation of marriage (Matt. 19:12).[23] That's because marriage is a special kind of communion between one man and one woman that is ordered toward their mutual love and toward the procreation of children—*bonding* and *babies*.

In 1930, Pope Pius XI wrote an encyclical on Christian marriage, *Casti Connubii*, which says that "the child holds the first place" as a blessing in marriage. Second is "the blessing of conjugal honor which consists in the mutual fidelity of the spouses in fulfilling the marriage contract" (19).

This understanding of marriage is not merely a "Catholic thing." It is universal, a part of our human nature. All cultures in human history recognized, until about two seconds ago, historically speaking, that marriage is a union of man and woman ordered to children and families. As the *Catechism* says:

The vocation to marriage is written in the very nature of man and woman as they came from the hand of the Creator. Marriage is not a purely human institution despite the many variations it may have undergone through the centuries in different cultures, social structures, and spiritual attitudes (1603).

Everybody's "Imposing"

People who claim that the Church is "imposing" its view of marriage on others don't realize that anyone who claims to define marriage for himself also "imposes" a view of marriage.

For example, laws that define marriage as "the union of two adults" impose that view on polygamists and those who believe in child brides (both of which are practices that, unlike SSM, actually have historical precedent). Civil and military courts that punish adultery impose their definition on those who don't believe that marriage is meant to be exclusive and faithful. In fact, the only way *not* to impose a definition of marriage is to say that marriage is "what anyone wants it to be"—in which case it ceases to be anything at all.

NOT JUST CHRISTIANS

Christianity did not exist until a little over 2,000 years ago, and yet, until just 2001 when the Netherlands became the first to legalize "gay marriage," the entire history of the pagan and non-Christian world had only known bride-and-groom marriages. Neither ancient cultures that approved of homosexuality nor modern atheistic regimes that are fiercely opposed to religion had or have "gay marriage." Why? Because the natural-law understanding of marriage (conjugal union of bride and bridegroom, woman and man) has always been a universal *human* understanding.

The conjugal view of marriage is the only view that explains why government has an interest in regulating marriage in the first place: because it's the only type of union that produces a child. This type of relationship is unique among all others, and society rightly sees the need to bind fathers to mothers formally, in order to secure and promote a stable environment in which to rear and educate children born from their union.

If we are going to accept the new "relational" or "romantic" view of marriage (that marriage is solely about the love that exists between two people), then none of the remaining marital norms that almost everyone—including supporters of SSM—accepts should still apply, such as:

Government Recognition. As much as it hurts to be lonely, most people would agree that it's not the government's job to make sure we have friends or to promote or regulate our intimate relationships. Government *can*, however, regulate the special conjugal relationship that exists between a man and a woman, because that relationship is capable of *public effects*. According to the CDF: "[Because] married couples ensure the succession of generations and are therefore eminently within the public interest, civil law grants them institutional recognition. Homosexual unions, on the other hand, do not need specific attention from the legal standpoint since they do not exercise this function for the common good."[24]

Permanence. If marriage were solely about affirming adult relationships and romantic love, then there would be no reason for the state to promote its permanence. Only the conjugal view of marriage explains why it's in the best interests of society to foster marital permanence; namely, because children are one of marriage's permanent effects. (The need for permanence will become even more clear when we talk about divorce.)

Monogamy. As Justice John Roberts noted in his dissent to *Obergefell*, according to the romantic view there is no logical reason to limit the definition of marriage to a *two-person* union. This is not an academic point. According to some researchers, there are as many as 500,000 polyamorous unions in the United States, and some of those groupings have applied for marriage licenses.[25] Though most proponents of SSM say they oppose polygamy and polyamory, according to their own principles there is no reason why they should.

Conjugality. If marriage is only about the bonds of love, then why couldn't a father and son, two elderly sisters, or two longtime bowling buddies have their relationship called "marriage"? Most people understand that these relationships are not marriages because they are not (and should not be) sexual, and sexual union is an essential part of marriage. Why has sex always and everywhere been understood to be an essential part of marriage, so much so that even civil marriages can be declared null for lack of consummation? It's because marriage is the only proper context for sex, the act that creates new human beings who form families, the foundation of society.

Sex and Marriage

You may be wondering why we are talking about same-sex marriage right after we discussed premarital sex. They may not seem similar, but these two issues are related for one reason: if people don't understand what *sex is for* then they won't understand what *marriage is for.*

Marriage isn't *only* for having children, because infertile persons may marry (as long as they can consummate), and married couples who become infertile don't stop being married. Instead, marriage is for the sexual union of man and woman, which is ordered toward the creation of children and the unification of the spouses. In other words, *marriage is for the marital act and the marital act only belongs in marriage.*

When people think that marriage is simply for companionship or romantic love, they have a hard time understanding why companionship and romance between same-sex couples should not be recognized as a marriage. They also don't understand why sex should be saved for marriage when marriage is just about a fuzzy concept of "love" rather than a one-flesh union that is ordered to result in a child.

However, when we recognize that only a man and woman can form the "one-flesh" bodily union of marriage, any relationship that lacks this element, no matter how dedicated or caring it may be, is not a marriage.

This is not a politically correct thing to say. But we must teach our children not to lie and not to *go along with a lie*, because the truth matters. That is why we must help our children walk through this cultural minefield by teaching them the truth about marriage. They will then be able to talk about marriage to peers who, in many cases, have known nothing but a lie.

REMEMBER...

- Marriage is the union of a man and a woman that is ordered toward their good as a couple and the procreation and education of any children born from that union.

- Marriage is not a mere "religious construct" but a part of our universal human nature whose fundamental elements the state cannot legitimately change.

- Only the conjugal or "man-woman" view of marriage explains why government has an interest in regulating marriage.

SAME-SEX MARRIAGE
Advice for Little Kids

I was ladling some soup for my kindergartener one afternoon when he said casually, but a bit tentatively, "Mom, girls can marry girls."

I knew this moment was coming. "Gay marriage" was not even an issue when my oldest children were little, but after the Supreme Court forced my hand, I knew I'd have to discuss it with my younger children.

I turned to my son, made eye contact with him, and replied in a calm voice, "Hmmm. Well, no, girls can't marry girls, sweetie. Where did you hear that they could?"

"Katie said they can."

"No, hon'. Katie is a nice little girl, but she is wrong. Only boys can marry girls. That's how God made families—with mommies and daddies marrying and then having babies. It is always very sad when little boys and girls don't have a mom or a dad, isn't it? So, even though you might hear strange things about marriage from your friends, or their parents, or even in the news, what you heard is not correct."

Man's Law and God's Law

Ideally, and in accord with what the Church teaches, we shouldn't talk about "gay marriage" or homosexuality with our little ones unless it's necessary.

We should do our best to protect our children's innocence and not put them in a situation where they will be exposed to a distortion of marital love, be it same-sex attractions, polyamory, cohabitation, or the like. Sometimes this means making difficult choices that will result in our being socially shamed and rejected, which is why (if we are honest) many parents start to go along with the culture instead of gently but courageously speaking out against it.

If the issue becomes unavoidable (e.g., an uncle or sister is getting "married" to a person of the same sex), we should simply speak about God's law being a very good thing, and how sad it is when the people who make the civil laws forget this. You might say:

> Lots of times, adults who make the country's laws make mistakes. Sometimes they are really confused and make very bad mistakes, like when they allowed slavery and abortion. But we are Catholic and we aren't confused, so we have to stick with the way God has always wanted things. The way he made us is for a lady and a man to get married and have babies. If we do things God's way, people are happy.

It's important for our children to see us interact graciously and kindly with people who disagree with fundamental aspects of our faith. If your child faces hostility at school or in the neighborhood for speaking the truth that "girls can't marry girls," you can explain to your child that attacks often come from people who have deep hurts in their own lives. Tell them, and show them, that it's possible to speak against lies without personally attacking the people who have been misled by those lies.

FORCING OUR VIEWS?

As your kids get older, they might hear from their friends that we shouldn't make laws that force our religion on other people. You can agree with that in cases of specifically Catholic doctrine: "Yes! We should never have a law that says every citizen must go to Mass!" However, the laws in every country should be in harmony with God's *moral* law, which applies to everyone, including non-Christians, and this is why we have laws against stealing and murdering. Laws exist to protect everyone's basic rights—like the right to life, or a child's right to have a relationship with his mom and dad—so that society, which is dependent on healthy families, can flourish!

Back to Mom and Dad

After our talk, my son seemed satisfied, understanding the need for children to have both a mother and a father, and he began to eat the soup that I had placed in front of him. My answers made sense to him. A child's heart unburdened by sin and untainted by error recognizes and accepts truth easily.

But other children, who have been wrongly taught or exposed to grave sin, might not have as easy a time understanding this, and they may push the issue with your kids. They may insist that "love is love" and that only a mean, hateful person would oppose letting people who love each other get married. You can remind your own child that *most* people love other people without marrying them:

Even though you love Daddy, does that mean you could marry Daddy? No, that's silly! Of course mommies and daddies love each other, and we should all love one another, but marriage is for the special love only mommies and daddies have that can make a new baby to come into the world.

The culture conditions us to believe that all family structures are equal, even though, deep down, we know this is not true. Even people in secular Europe (where only about ten percent of Catholics attend Mass) understand this primal right of children to be raised by their married mom and dad.

NOT THE NORM

Remind your children that, even though it may seem like SSM is the norm (they won't remember a time without it), it wasn't always that way. For all of history up until a few years ago, the whole world—even non-Catholics and people who don't believe in God—knew that ladies only marry men, and grooms only have brides (not another groom!), and that this was very good. Point out how strange it is that, just recently, a few people wanted to change the law in a really big hurry, and now they tell us that the world's age-old understanding of marriage is *bad*! Your children will get that something there is just not right.

Case in point: a few years ago, a million French citizens took to the streets in protest of SSM. They marched under the banner of "children need a mother and a father" and were led by two prominent gay French citizens, including Frigide Barjot, a flamboyant lesbian comedian who generally supports rights for same-sex couples. She told the *New York Times*, "The problem is not homosexuality, but human filiation . . . . To make a child, you need a man and a woman."[26] Other protesters who joined her at the Eiffel Tower carried signs that read, "Mother and father, it's best for the child." Anyone is capable of loving a child or being a caretaker, but nothing can replace the unique and complementary gifts that mothers and fathers provide to children.

Finally, let your children know that upholding the natural view of marriage is not about pitting *people* against one another, but about two competing—and irreconcilable—views of marriage: one that is solely about what adult people desire for themselves, and the other that serves the needs and protects the rights of children by uniting a man and woman in a permanent, monogamous bond—a bond naturally designed to welcome and nurture the new life it produces.

REMEMBER . . .

- Make decisions about schooling, friends, and media that protect your child's natural innocence.

- If the issue becomes unavoidable, talk about how sad it is when people don't understand marriage and why mommies and daddies are so important.

- Remind your older "little kids" that marriage is a universal human norm from God and nature, and not something that the Church made up to force on everyone.

SAME-SEX MARRIAGE
Advice for Big Kids

When it comes to helping teenagers think through this issue, your main task will be to answer their questions and
help them see that it isn't "bigoted" to defend natural marriage. Questions may come from challenges their friends or
teachers pose, but your child may also be struggling with the
issue himself, or even be in favor of same-sex marriage and
want to challenge you.

Above all else, remind your child about the natural-law
principles we discussed earlier, and try to bring the conversation back to the questions, *"What is marriage?"* and *"What
is marriage for?"*

The "Free to Love" Objection

Common questions from teens today are, "Why are you
against love?" and "Why can't people who love each other
get married?"

Such questions are understandable, as almost every young
person today believes that marriage is first and foremost about
"love"—in the sense of romantic feelings. To reorient your
child's mindset, remind him that throughout the history of

the world, feelings of love have never been a prerequisite for marriage. No couple has ever had to prove they are in love to get a marriage license.

Don't get me wrong! Romantic feelings between spouses are wonderful and ideal, but they've never been required for a valid marriage. If they had, then generations of marriages throughout history would not be "real" marriages—including tens of millions of consensual arranged marriages, which still occur today.

My grandparents were married long ago in the "old country," and they did not know each other well when they became husband and wife. Yet the bishop presided at their nuptial Mass, family and friends celebrated heartily, and their marriage lasted for over fifty years, until Grandpa died. Their marriage produced six children, fourteen grandchildren, myriad great-grandchildren, and now their great-great grandchildren have started to arrive! Would anyone claim that Grandma and Grandpa were never *really* married?

If your teen continues to insist that a "feeling" of love is essential for true marriage, ask him how far we should take this principle:

- If three or four people all "feel" romantic love for each other, does it mean that group can be married?

- If siblings, or a mother and son, have romantic feelings for each other, should they be allowed to marry?

- Should government officials somehow make people prove they "love each other" before issuing a marriage license?

- When spouses "fall out of love," does their marriage suddenly cease to exist?

If the answer to any of these questions is "no," then your child cannot say that marriage is just a matter of "love is love," or that romantic feelings are the basis for marriage. In defining something, we must find out what is universal about the thing we are defining. This common quality (or *essence*) is what makes it that particular "thing" and not any other "thing."

Every culture in history has recognized that the essence of marriage—its common recognizable quality—is its conjugal nature. In other words, marriage occurs when a man and woman publicly make a promise of permanent union to one another and subsequently consummate their marriage through sexual intercourse.[27]

The "Infertility" Objection

You may also hear this challenge: "You say that marriage is inherently about making babies, but then why are infertile men and women allowed to get married?" This question implicitly argues that same-sex couples should be treated like infertile male/female couples; however, the two categories are radically different in kind, and so they should not be treated as if they were the same.

Infertility means that the reproductive system—the only human biological system that requires union with another person to be complete—is broken or aged beyond its years of function. A couple is considered infertile when they engage in the act that naturally procreates children yet are consistently unable to conceive a child. A same-sex couple can never be called *infertile* because they are not engaging in *that act*. The things they do with each other are never, by their nature, ordered to procreation. Their "unions" are barren by nature's design.

The sexual union of a man and a woman, on the other hand, is *always* ordered toward procreation, even if the couple does not actually conceive a child due to age or medical disorders. In most cases we can't say which bride and groom will be childless, and there are married couples who unexpectedly conceive after many years of infertility. But even for couples known to be completely infertile at the time of marriage—for example, where the woman has had a hysterectomy—the marital act still expresses the ends for which it was made. Remember that it's not the conceiving of children that makes a marriage valid (because we do not have ultimate control over conception), but rather the ability to unite totally in a one-flesh union of husband and wife.[28]

BASEBALL, MARRIAGE, AND PROPER DEFINITIONS

Here's an analogy drawn from the book *What is Marriage?* that explains why infertile couples can marry but same-sex couples cannot.[29]

What makes a baseball team a baseball team is that the players are ordered toward the goal of winning baseball games. Yet even if they don't win a single game, they are still a baseball team and can achieve goods like teamwork even if they don't achieve victories. On the other hand, nine men hitting baseballs and catching pop flies for the fun of it may pursue goods like friendship, but they are not a baseball team. This isn't because the nine guys haven't won any games, it's because the activity they're engaged in isn't ordered toward the goal of winning games.

Likewise, the conjugal union between a man and a woman is the *only union*—the only game in town!—where two bodies become one, in a function that can create new life. That *unique* union, even when not fertile, is the essential and indispensable element of marriage.

The "Discrimination" Objection

Explain to your teen that everyone "discriminates," because to discriminate just means *to choose among options* (as in "discriminating tastes"). Now, *unjust* discrimination means "treating equals unequally," but same-sex couples are not equal to opposite-sex couples.

This is something that even secular people and civil law implicitly understand. For example, in both civil and religious law, non-consummation has always been a grounds for nullity of marriage. The secular government of the United Kingdom officially admits the inherent rule: "You can annul a marriage if it wasn't consummated—you haven't had sex with the person you married since the wedding . . ." Yet, then we see this telling caveat in parentheses: "*(doesn't apply for same-sex couples).*"[30] Of course, that's because same-sex couples cannot physically consummate a marriage, cannot *actually* have sex.

A government can't legitimately establish two completely different sets of rules for what we all are forced to declare "the same." If a same-sex couple cannot play by the same (equal) rules as a husband and wife, then "marriage equality" is a ruse from the start.

MARRIAGE AND LEGAL BENEFITS

Some folks claim that same-sex couples are harmed when they don't have the same legal benefits married couples have, like hospital visitation rights or inheritance claims. But the government *could* give legal benefits to any household or couple it chooses, even if those citizens were in a non-sexual relationship (e.g., siblings who cohabit, or committed friends). What the government *cannot* legitimately do (even though it has claimed to) is redefine a universal institution written into our human nature that it did not create or define in the first place.

Activists for SSM quickly moved past "civil unions" and other such arrangements for same-sex relationships because legal benefits were never the real goal. Full acceptance and social *legitimacy* of their relationships was the desired outcome, something that could only come about if their pairings were called "marriage."

The "Gay Marriage Doesn't Affect You" Objection

When the other objections are answered, it may still come down to, "How does gay marriage affect you anyway?"

Well, aside from egregious infringement upon religious liberties and rights of conscience that forces Christian store owners and Catholic charities to facilitate same-sex marriages on pain of crippling fines, business closures, and even jail sentences,[31] redefining marriage has another effect: it weakens and destabilizes all marriages.

We can't radically change the meaning of a thing, inverting or contradicting its very nature, without harming it. Marriage is a pre-political, universal institution that has always had a specific character (conjugal union of bride and groom) and meaning (procreation and education of children). Promoting SSM means supporting the falsehood that marriage is a state-determined validation of any kind of feelings-based relationship whose fluctuating norms are determined solely by the adults involved.

With this kind of laxity in definition and understanding, there is little to nothing left that we all agree is "marriage." Why even have marriage at all? No surprise, then, that the International Social Survey Program found that in countries where SSM was made legal, more than half the people believe that marriage is an "outdated institution."[32]

And when marriage is weakened or undermined, family and society begin to free-fall. Your teen can simply look around and see.

Life in a Post-Obergefell World

Because few people in our culture understand natural law or accept the concept of objective truth, we can't expect our arguments to turn back the clock and restore marriage to its proper place in law and society. In fact, faithful Catholics and other defenders of natural marriage are now mocked and derided (and legislated against) at every turn, and the opposition to truth is only getting stronger. The "dictatorship of relativism" that Pope Benedict XVI talked about is real.[33] We must teach our teens to be willing to be the outliers, standing up for what's right—even if it's unpopular, and even if we are punished and rejected as harshly as Christ was (John 15:18). Christ calls us to this kind of heroism, and he does not ask his disciples to suffer any pain or humiliation that he has not already suffered.

Our teens also need to know that, along with logical arguments, our most important evidence will be our own marriages. A common refrain when Christians explain the injustice and disorder that comes with acceptance of "gay marriage" is, "But what about the way Christians have destroyed the meaning of marriage with widespread acceptance of divorce? That is far more harmful!" That astute observation is why we now must address a previous redefinition of marriage that came with "no-fault" divorce. Divorce declares the intrinsically *permanent* state of marriage as "non-permanent," a catastrophic reversal that gave SSM and other re-definitions a foothold.

REMEMBER...

- The natural definition of marriage does not prevent anyone from loving anyone else, and we all discriminate (choose between one thing or another). It's only *unjust* discrimination that is morally wrong, and there are just reasons for the natural definition of marriage.

- Marriage is for the particular sexual union that only a man and a woman can achieve, ordered toward the procreation of children. Infertile couples can marry because they can still consummate a marriage (partake in the marital act), which is something same-sex couples cannot do. There is no other relationship on earth like it, which is why marriage is the foundation of every society.

- Our children will have to live out a courageous view of marriage in a world that is increasingly confused about men (husbands and fathers), women (wives and mothers), children, and how they should relate to one another.

5

DIVORCE
What the Church Teaches

As a Catholic, I have always been "against" divorce, but Church teaching on the issue didn't really reach my heart until I published *Primal Loss: The Now-Adult Children of Divorce Speak*. The heartbreaking words of seventy contributors reveal the painful, long-lasting effects of divorce on children. Here's how one of them describes her parents' divorce, which took place more than forty years earlier:

> I was devastated as a child when my dad drove away, and I will never forget standing in our front yard literally screaming, "Come back!" I didn't understand what was happening, and my three-year-old sister certainly didn't understand. I remember my grandma (my mom's mom) grabbing me, telling me he loved other women and to stop screaming . . . . I "survived" the divorce, but the fallout wasn't pretty: lots of acting out and "unsettled" behavior. It really skewed the way I looked at guys and what I thought "love" was. If marriage wasn't forever, why should anything else be?[34]

The Plague of Divorce

But the evil of divorce begins before the harms it does to children. It is an evil in itself because it

> claims to break the contract, to which the spouses freely consented, to live with each other till death. Divorce does injury to the covenant of salvation, of which sacramental marriage is the sign. Contracting a new union, even if it is recognized by civil law, adds to the gravity of the rupture: the remarried spouse is then in a situation of public and permanent adultery (CCC 2384).

The Bible tells us that God literally *hates divorce* (Mal. 2:16), and because marriage is a natural-law issue (not strictly a religious observance), all people are morally bound to respect the natural permanence of the marital bond. Not just Catholics, but anyone who can reason, can see that divorce, which is an attempt to break the marital contract, constitutes a "grave offense against the natural law" (CCC 2384).

Divorce is a "grave offense" that causes "grave harm" and leaves "children traumatized." But divorce doesn't just harm the couple and their children; it harms *society*. Divorce "introduces disorder into the family and society" (CCC 2385), rendering them unable to flourish and, in what the *Catechism* calls a "contagious effect," radiates its harms far past the couple, making it "truly a plague on society." Yes, the *Catechism* actually identifies divorce as a contagious plague!

Let's remember that, in many cases, one spouse wants to end the marriage while the other wants to remain faithful to the vows. In those cases, the committed spouse is not guilty of the sin of divorce, but is a victim of it (CCC 2386). The

Church stresses that "[divorce] brings grave harm to the deserted spouse and to children traumatized by the separation of their parents and often torn between them" (CCC 2385).

WHAT ABOUT ANNULMENTS?

Unlike divorce, which attempts to dissolve a valid marriage, a declaration of nullity is a judicial finding that there was never a valid marriage in the first place. It *appeared* the couple was married on their wedding day, but a necessary element of marriage was missing. There may have been impediments like fraud, coercion, or an inability to fully consent that kept the marital union from coming into being. Annulments are thus not the "Catholic version of divorce." We should also note that invalid marriages can often be regularized through the process of convalidation.

Separation and Legal Issues

But what about marriages where there is ongoing, unrepentant adultery? Or when a spouse or the children are in danger? May the victimized spouse and the children leave the home? Absolutely, and the Church allows for physical separation in those cases: "The separation of spouses while maintaining the marriage bond can be legitimate in certain cases provided for by canon law" (CCC 2383).*

---

* In some very rare cases the Church tolerates civil divorce, but "tolerance" does not mean acceptance. Even after a civil divorce is filed, a hope for a restoration of the marriage must remain and the couple must still uphold their vows, including the vow of fidelity, and not engage in a new romantic relationship or contract a new civil marriage while the previous marriage is still presumed valid in the eyes of the Church.

The *Catechism* says that divorce "claims to break the contract, to which the spouses freely consented, to live with each other till death" (2384). Notice the phrase, "claims to break." It can get confusing, because we use the same word ("divorce" and "civil divorce") when we are speaking of two different concepts—the former forbidden and the latter sometimes "tolerated." Christ clearly forbids divorce (the attempt to break the marriage contract), and the Church teaches that divorce is a grave violation of natural law—a sin.

So, how can it be that some divorce is "tolerated" by the Church? A civil divorce may be tolerated if it's "the only possible way of ensuring certain legal rights" and protections for victimized spouses and children, *but not if one approaches the civil court in an attempt to break the marriage contract, which is always immoral.*[35]

It would be better to call civil divorce "defensive legal maneuvering" instead. Why? Because the Church presumes that married couples are in valid marriages, and those marriages remain perfectly valid *even after* a civil divorce decree. The state's decree of divorce cannot nullify the bond— whether natural or sacramental—formed by the couple's vow. Even if conjugal living cannot be restored and a couple ends up remaining apart and civilly divorced, the marriage bond remains until death.

The Impossibility of Divorce

Jesus tells us that a Christian husband and wife are "no longer two but one flesh. What therefore God has joined together, let not man put asunder" (Matt. 19:6; cf. Mark 10:9). According to the *Catechism*, "The Lord Jesus insisted on the original intention of the Creator who willed that marriage be indissoluble. . . . Between the baptized, 'a ratified and consummated marriage cannot be dissolved by any human power or for any reason other than death'" (2382).* Marriage is made not only to be a union between one man and one woman, but to be a *permanent* union between them until death.

St. Paul teaches that "the wife should not separate from her husband" and "the husband should not divorce his wife." But if this does happen, and even if a person is divorced against his will (and therefore not morally culpable for the sin of divorce), then one must remain single or be reconciled to one's spouse (1 Cor. 7:10–11). What a civilly divorced person *cannot* do is marry another person while the first spouse is still alive. Neither civil divorce nor abandonment affects the permanence of the marital bond, which St. Paul makes clear in Romans 7:2-3:

> A married woman is bound by law to her husband as long as he lives; but if her husband dies she is discharged from the law concerning the husband. Accordingly, she will be called an adulteress if she lives with another man while her husband is alive. But if her husband dies she is free from that law, and if she marries another man she is not an adulteress.

Jesus, too, did not mince words: "Everyone who divorces his wife and marries another commits adultery, and he who marries a woman divorced from her husband commits adultery" (Luke 16:18; cf. Mark 10:6-8). So divorce itself is a sin, and a remarriage constitutes the added sin of adultery. As the *Catechism* says, "Contracting a new union, even if it is recognized by civil law, adds to the gravity of the rupture:

---

* A valid *natural* marriage, in which one or both spouses is unbaptized, is indissoluble in that the couple may not dissolve the bond themselves. In certain rare circumstances, however, the Church may apply either the so-called *Pauline Privilege* or *Petrine Privilege* to dissolve such a non-sacramental union "in favor of the Faith."

the remarried spouse is then in a situation of public and permanent adultery" (2384).

Rejoice and Be Glad!

For many people, these words of Jesus are hard to follow, especially in our divorce culture and most especially for those who have been personally involved in a divorce. But victims of divorce should not reject Jesus' words out of cynicism, and perpetrators of divorce should not reject these words out of guilt. If we reject God's condemnation of divorce, then we also reject his promise that love never fails (1 Cor. 13:8) and that we can do all things in Christ who strengthens us (Phil. 4:13).

Instead, we should rejoice that the Catholic Church has, almost entirely alone, upheld Jesus' teaching about marriage. His teaching protects spouses, children, extended families, and the order of society itself. However, in order to experience the true joy of this teaching, we must overcome any doubts we might have about God's plan for marriage. We must teach our children—who live in a generation of broken families—how to understand with compassion the sin of divorce, while also standing firmly and graciously for the permanent nature of marriage.

REMEMBER . . .

- Divorce violates the natural permanence of marriage and causes grave harm.

- God hates divorce, and Christian marriage can only be dissolved by the death of one of the spouses.

- Christ's teaching on marriage is hard, but every cross embraced leads to holiness, peace, and joy.

DIVORCE

Advice for Little Kids

My son John was a twelve-year-old sixth-grader when he hopped into my car after school and said, "Carl's parents are getting a divorce. He's been crying during class, and it's really sad. He can't even do his schoolwork."

I knew from the seventy people I interviewed for *Primal Loss* what Carl's next months, years, and decades were going to look like. I wanted to find his parents, knock some sense into them, and beg them to change course. According to my son, Carl continued to spiral downward, and this once-happy boy was now leaving school early several times each month to see a therapist.

It was difficult for John to watch his buddy suffer as the breakup unfolded, yet this was not my son's first exposure to divorce. In fact, whereas exactly none of my public grade-school classmates in the 1970s came from divorced homes, my children tell me that about half of their peers—in public, charter, and Catholic schools—are children of divorce. Our kids are growing up in a divorce culture, and there is no shielding their innocence on this issue.

So, when our young children hear of friends' parents or their own relatives who are divorced or divorcing, what do we say?

Discussing Divorce

For little ones who are hearing about divorce for the first time, we must explain, simply and with a heavy heart, what it is: "Divorce is when one or both people who are married decide that they don't want to be married anymore, and so they don't live together in the same house after that."

We also must explain why divorce is wrong while being sensitive to the fact that those who are divorced are often people your child looks up to, such as a friend's parents or beloved relatives. For that reason, it's important to distinguish between the *act* we condemn and the *person* we love.

Let's consider one example of how this conversation might go, using an all-too common scenario: explaining why grandparents are divorced.

"Mommy, why isn't Grandpa married to Grandma? Isn't he Daddy's daddy, and isn't Grandma Daddy's mommy?"

> Yes, honey, and it's so very sad that Grandma and Grandpa don't live together anymore like they used to! Sometimes grownups get divorced because they think they will be happier not living together anymore. They might not realize how sad it makes God when marriages and families break apart. But God knows what will really make us happy and that's why we should listen to him.

There is no need to give a small child explicit details or dwell on things that may have contributed to a couple's divorce. If you think your child may become worried about God being mad at loved ones for getting divorced, talk about how God never stops loving us. You might say:

> Sometimes grown-ups don't know God very well, and sometimes they just don't want to listen to him. Do

you know what we should do? Let's pray for them! God will always listen to our prayers, and he especially loves to hear and respond to the prayers of children. God loves Grandpa and Grandma even more than we do, and he wants us to pray for them always. Let's pray that God will help our hearts be pure just like his, and that no matter what happens, we can all be together in heaven together one day.

THE VICTIMS OF DIVORCE

We should remind children that divorce isn't always a mutual decision. This helps them be empathetic toward those who are the victims of divorce and not rush to the conclusion that every divorced person doesn't care about God's laws. You might say:

"Remember that [the husband or wife] may not have wanted to break apart the marriage at all! But in America today, the courts will not let someone stay married if the other person wants to leave the marriage and break up the family. That is very sad, and it's not fair to the kids *or* to the spouse who wants to stay together as a family. Let's pray that God will heal their hurting hearts and give them his peace."

Standing up to Divorce

Let me say something a bit controversial: it's *okay* to let your child see a spark of righteous anger when you hear of yet another divorce.

Children totally depend on the adults in their lives for protection (of which an intact marriage is the greatest), but in the case of divorce at least one of the parents has withdrawn that protection. Divorce is always an injustice to a child, and the divorce of a friend's parents can reasonably strike fear in the hearts of our own kids. If you are married, make your child feel safe ("Dad [Mom] and I will never get divorced, so you don't have to worry about that, ever!"), and show your fierce opposition to what is happening to children of divorce.

If you are a divorced parent, be honest with your children about what happened without going into explicit or inappropriate detail. If you did not want the divorce, you are in the best position to confirm the evils of divorce, and your children will need you to validate their pain. If you were the one who abandoned your marriage, there is forgiveness after repentance, but you must do your best to make it up to your children, acknowledging the pain you have caused, with no excuses or caveats.

Whatever your personal experiences may be, do not let other parents' or adults' perceptions of you deter you from standing firm on this issue. Children's welfare and the future of marriage are more important than any critical comments you might hear from others.

Is Divorce a Good Thing?

Occasionally, your child might float out an alleged benefit of divorce that he has heard from a classmate: "Kristie says it's really cool having two Christmases and two birthdays— double the gifts!"

Although some divorced adults promote a bright side of divorce, it's not comforting in the long run. Explain to your child that having Mom and Dad together in a secure home is better than constantly moving between two homes while getting extra material "stuff." As one now-adult child of divorce told me:

We kids wanted our parents to be happy growing up. We bragged that we had two houses, multiple Christmases, and bigger families to love us. We said we wouldn't trade it for anything despite the difficulties. As an adult, I would definitely trade it for married parents and a stable household. I would rather have seen my parents grow and mature and stick it out than continue this lifetime of arduous and seemingly impossible family blending.[36]

The trauma of a shattered family is made worse when we minimize the pain of divorce. Remember Carl? His mom told him that the divorce was "no big deal," invalidating the searing pain that children like Carl naturally feel—which is a very big deal indeed. As Melody, a now-adult child of divorce, has written, "If, as all the adults around me were saying, divorce was 'good,' 'better,' and 'best,' and if my parents were wholly justified and excellent decision-makers, then *I* must have been a worthless person for all the sadness, grief, and anger I carried."[37]

Only as an adult did Melody realize that her overwhelming grief and confusion in childhood were not wrong. She now tells us that what she *should have* heard from counselors, teachers, and priests as a child (but never did) was this:

What happened between your mom and dad was bad. Families are made to love one another forever and that didn't happen in yours. Your family was dismantled without your consent. And now you are left with an anger and sorrow that are justified. Everything you are feeling is *normal*. The path you're walking now involves growing through this pain and even thriving in the midst of it. God can bring joy out of suffering if we give our hearts to him, and I will walk with you on this journey so you don't have to face it alone.

Let's make sure that the children of divorce hear *this* message and not the message of "no big deal." No matter the circumstances, whether high-conflict or "good divorce," the child will still need to mourn the loss of his family, and we must respect and acknowledge that it will take years and even a lifetime to heal from this foundational trauma and grief.

Equipped with all of these truths, your own children will be able to empathize with friends who are facing or have experienced the divorce of their parents, while never minimizing or condoning the injustice those friends have endured.

REMEMBER . . .

- You should frame the discussion of divorce around the sadness that comes from not following God's plan for marriage.

- Remind your children that we always pray for people who have experienced divorce and that not everyone who is divorced wanted it to happen.

- If you instigated a divorce, be honest with your children and humbly ask for forgiveness in order to begin the path to healing and reconciliation.

DIVORCE

Advice for Big Kids

One of Trent's friends confided in him about an experience he had visiting his father who had left him when he was five and moved across the world. As a result of the divorce, his family fell into poverty and had to move into a dilapidated house with rooms that didn't even have drywall. When his father saw him again during his teen years he asked his son, "What was I supposed to do? Did you want me to be unhappy for the rest of my life?"

His son immediately blurted back, "Yes! You should have been there for us!"

Our teens are torn by the question of divorce. On the one hand, many of them have seen and even experienced the trauma it causes, and they instinctively hear their consciences saying that it's wrong. On the other hand, teens are bombarded by our culture's message that what matters most is "being happy and fulfilled." If that's true, then isn't it best to "move on" from a rocky marriage and seek out a new partner who will make us happy?

Our task is to show our teens that real happiness flows from a sacrificial love and that divorce doesn't free us to find "true love"—it *kills* true love.

Promote "Marriage Equality"

Start with the basics and explain to your child that the purpose of marriage is to create a *family,* comprising relationships that cannot be ended in this life. I can decide that I'm no longer friends with someone, but I can't decide that my sister is no longer my sister or that I'm no longer my parents' daughter. The marriage bond (by God's design!) produces and undergirds these biological connections.

The unbreakable bond of husband and wife exists for a reason. Consider that when a child is born, he is completely helpless. In God's perfect design, *biology* ensures that the baby's mother is right there to help and protect him and *matrimony* ensures that the baby's father is right there to help and protect both of them.

In fact, the bond of matrimony is even stronger than the bond of biology, for it continues even after the child leaves his parents' home. Marriage is made by God to be the strongest human bond there is, precisely because its nature is to create, protect, and nurture a family.

As Trent's story illustrates, when we break this sacred bond we betray the family with devastating effect. The current generation of young people has been raised with the concept of "equality" as sacrosanct, so show your teen how divorce sets up children for a lifetime of inequality.[38] This is evident in the decades of social science research confirming that children are almost always physically, emotionally, and financially worse off after divorce:

- Children of divorce are more likely to develop asthma, cancer, have problems with substance abuse and be physically or sexually abused.[39] A study that began in 1921 concluded that "parental divorce during childhood was the single strongest social predictor of early death, many years into the future."[40]

- Children of divorce are more likely to receive diagnoses of depression, aggressiveness, and bipolar disorder.[41] They are also more likely to abandon their faith, have earlier sexual experiences, with girls eight times more likely to become pregnant in their teens.[42]

- Divorced women are more likely to lose their health insurance and have their incomes fall below the poverty line.[43] Children of single-parent homes are the least likely to improve their economic situations when they enter adulthood.[44]

- Children of divorce are forty percent more likely to have their own marriages end in divorce.[45] Children with parents who remarry are ninety-one percent more likely to get divorced, thus perpetuating this devastating cycle of trauma.[46]

In an address to the Catholic Medical Association, Peter Kreeft pointed out that if some food or activity caused this much harm to families it would be regulated if not completely outlawed. But, as he put it, "divorce is tolerated and accepted because it's about sex."[47]

So ask your teens, "Why is marriage the only legal contract that one party can unilaterally break for any reason? And is it right that the one who wishes to honor the contract *loses* in court 100 percent of the time? Why do we expect people to keep their sacred and legal promises in other contexts, but in the most important promise we make—a marriage vow—we accept and even encourage its violation?"

CONNECT THE DOTS

Teens—and even adults—often don't connect a young person's problems with their divorced parents, because we're told, over and over, that children are "resilient." If one of your child's classmates starts "cutting," becomes depressed, or starts experimenting with "gender fluidity" and homosexual acts, and their parents are divorced or are getting a divorce, don't be afraid to ask your child, "Do you think the break-up of his family might have something to do with his behavior?"

One friend, a child of divorce herself, points out to her kids each instance of divorce-related dysfunction, laying the blame directly on that sin. She will say things like, "Oh, no, honey, your cousin won't be at the family gathering, because she doesn't spend time at her dad's anymore. That's what divorce does; it breaks families apart, even extended families and cousins." Her children understand the devastation.

Divorce devastates financially, emotionally, and spiritually; it ends friendships, destroys relationships in the extended family, and forces even church communities to take sides. Being divorced against one's will harms psychological stability and sense of self-worth, makes it more difficult to love and feel lovable, and can cause great loneliness. Divorce decimates the next generation, too, taking an axe to the tree of life. There are very few things in the Bible that God is said explicitly to "hate" but, as we've seen, divorce is one of those things (Mal. 2:16).

Fidelity to the Truth

Explain to your child that just a few decades ago, society understood divorce to be a very bad thing. With bewildering speed we have since reversed our stance on the moral law, and now we call divorce good. It's been said that a society can survive its people doing evil things, but a society cannot survive its people calling evil good.

Repeat that to your child often, until it sinks in.

Mom or Dad's voice should be running through their heads, even as they grow into adulthood. I remember my own parents telling me more than once, "We don't believe in divorce!" So I knew that my family and my identity—my foundation—would always be secure, even during rough patches and difficult seasons. And I knew that when I got married, no matter what, that union was for life.

Let your children hear your words and know you mean them, and don't let your own past sins, or even your own divorced status, keep you from educating your children about the trauma of divorce. I have one dear friend (an abandoned spouse) who tells priests, "I am a divorced woman! My kids are sitting in the pews listening to you—please, please, tell them the truth about the evils of divorce!" By speaking the truth, by pointing out the damage divorce does, we inoculate our kids against divorce in their own futures.

Teens, especially the children of divorce, need to know that divorce is not predestined.

Even though they might be tempted to do so, they do not have to follow in their parents' footsteps. Their free will and all the little decisions they make every day determine their destiny. Your child (and you, too) have the power to choose to love within a marriage, day by day, even when love is not returned—and even for a long time. God's grace empowers us to love as he loves, without counting the cost, until death. Drive home to your children that God loves us when we are unlovable and when we do not love him. Indeed, "God shows his love for us in that while we were yet sinners Christ died for us" (Rom. 5:8).

God truly chose to love us "for better or for worse."

In our disposable, feelings-based world, your teens will find no better illustration of Christ's love on earth today than in a marriage relationship lived out in sacrificial love, with no promise retracted, no person discarded. If you teach your child about the sacrificial love of a marriage, being true to the other in good times and in bad, in sickness and in health, loving and honoring the other *all the days of one's life* (even if it's not reciprocated!), then you will have also taught him about the love of Christ for us.

REMEMBER...

- Marriage is a lifelong social bond because it secures the lifelong biological bonds that flow from the union of husbands and wives.

- Divorce wreaks havoc on the physical, mental, and spiritual health of the family. It should not be celebrated as a solution to the problems experienced in marriage.

- Don't be afraid to denounce the evil of divorce to your teens, especially if your family has been fractured by it. Through the grace of God, divorce does not have to be your children's destiny.

6

CONTRACEPTION
What the Church Teaches

A friendly young air conditioner technician came to my home a few years ago, and some small talk led to him asking, "So how many kids do you have, anyway?"

"We have eight."

He was startled and then began to chuckle, "Oh, are you crazy?!"

I was not offended and sensed that he had a good heart, so I laughed and said, "Well, two are in college, and so only six are in the house right now."

"We had three, and then I got fixed," he replied.

I didn't even hesitate and simply said with a smile, "Oh, were you broken?"

He answered with nervous laughter and some hesitation, not expecting me to question our culture's acceptance of a "fix" that causes a healthy bodily system to stop working.

Because we moderns have been thoroughly indoctrinated with the idea that contraception is the "responsible" thing (even for married couples), we must reorient our thinking on this subject—starting with how we got here in the first place.

The Road to Contraception

Contraception, like every other sin, is nothing new. Thousands of years ago, Greeks and Egyptians used plants and dung to make spermicides, and the Bible records a man named Onan engaging in *coitus interruptus* (a.k.a. the "withdrawal method") in order to avoid having a child—an act that was "displeasing in the sight of the Lord" (Gen. 38:9-10). Fallen human beings have always attempted to make their sexual acts barren, but even non-Christians have understood how this violates the moral law. Mahatma Gandhi, a Hindu, said that "if artificial [birth control] methods become the order of the day, nothing but moral degradation can be the result."[48]

From the time of Christ until the twentieth century, *all* Christian churches and even most secular authorities opposed contraception. This changed in 1930, when the Church of England rejected almost two millennia of Christian moral teaching and allowed contraceptive use, but only for married couples who had serious reasons. Fast-forward several decades, and today almost all Protestant denominations approve the use of contraception for any reason; not only permitting it, but calling it good. Many Catholics also think there's nothing wrong with contraception, which is ironic given that the modern contraceptive movement was spearheaded by a woman who hated Christianity.

In 1921, Margaret Sanger founded the American Birth Control League, which is now known as Planned Parenthood. Sanger wanted birth control to prevent people with "inferior genes" from reproducing, which was her solution for poverty. Sanger referred to the poor as "human weeds," "defective stock," and "the feeble-minded." She also criticized "religious scruples" that prevented people from "exercising control over their numbers." Her early pamphlets contained the chilling motto, "No gods, no masters."[49]

Sanger's movement grew more popular throughout the decades, and during the Sexual Revolution of the 1960s, the hormonal birth control pill arrived. Tragically, most Christian denominations touted it as a blessing for women and families, but the Catholic Church refused to go along with the spirit of the age. In 1968, Pope Paul VI reiterated the unbroken teaching of the Church on the immorality of contraception in his landmark encyclical, *Humanae Vitae*.

When we read what popes like Paul VI and John Paul II taught about contraception, we see that their intention is not, as many accuse, to "oppress women." Rather, their intention is to liberate women from objectification and prevent marriage from losing its sacred dignity. In fact, everything we know about the Church's teaching on premarital sex, divorce, and same-sex marriage dovetails beautifully with the Church's unbroken stance on contraceptives. See with the eyes of heaven: if marriage is for love (union and permanence) and life (procreation), then it would be wrong to sterilize a life-giving act of love.

A PAPAL PROPHET

In *Humanae Vitae*, Pope Paul VI made an accurate prediction about the consequences of contraceptive use:

"[It will] open wide the way for marital infidelity and a general lowering of moral standards. Not much experience is needed to be fully aware of human weakness and to understand that human beings—and especially the young, who are so exposed to temptation—need incentives to keep the moral law, and it is an evil thing to make it easy for them to break that law . . . . [A man will reduce a woman] to being a mere instrument for the satisfaction of his own desires, no longer considering her as his partner whom he should surround with care and affection" (17).

A Barrier to Becoming "One Flesh"

In sexual union, a married man and woman don't merely engage in an activity that is pleasurable and makes them feel emotionally closer to one another. In the act of marital love, husband and wife fully give themselves to each other in an act that makes them "one flesh" and is ordered toward the creation of a new human life. According to the *Catechism*:

> A child does not come from outside as something added on to the mutual love of the spouses, but springs from the very heart of that mutual giving, as its fruit and fulfillment. So the Church, which is "on the side of life," teaches that "it is necessary that each and every marriage act remain ordered *per se* to the procreation of human life (2366).

The love between spouses is fully expressed in the marital act because it expresses the full gift of each—body and soul—to the other. Anything less than that full gift is a misuse of the act.

If the man were to hold back his mind, for example, by thinking of another woman during sex, this would distort the unitive purpose of sex (they can't become one if his mind is with someone else). Likewise, if the woman makes it impossible for her husband to share in her fertility by blocking it with hormones or barriers, this distorts the procreative purpose of sex (they can't become one if they withhold from each other their bodies' powers of reproduction). The *Catechism*, quoting Pope Paul VI, says:

"By safeguarding both these essential aspects, the unitive and the procreative, the conjugal act preserves in its fullness the sense of true mutual love and its orientation toward man's exalted vocation to parenthood" . . . . "[E]very action which, whether in anticipation of the conjugal act, or in its accomplishment, or in the development of its natural consequences, proposes, whether as an end or as a means, to render procreation impossible" is intrinsically evil (CCC 2369-2370).

This does not mean that married couples can only have sex when they have the expressed intent to conceive a baby. After all, the Lord himself designed a woman's cycle to be made up of mostly non-fertile days, and of course women are not fertile while pregnant or after menopause. What it *does* mean is that whenever a couple does choose to have sex, they may not willfully sterilize the sexual act. Contraception is wrong because it tries to change the nature of the marital act, which is made by God and unchangeable. According to Pope St. John Paul II in *Familiaris Consortio* (FC):

The total reciprocal self-giving of husband and wife is overlaid, through contraception, by an objectively contradictory language, namely, that of not giving oneself totally to the other. This leads not only to a positive refusal to be open to life but also to a falsification of the inner truth of conjugal love, which is called upon to give itself in personal totality (32).

We can only say "the two have become one" when a husband and wife freely give their *whole selves* to each other in sexual intimacy. This is not possible if the couple is using contraception and essentially saying, "I want some of you, but not your fertility! Keep that away from me!"

How Do You Do It?

In my conversation with the air-conditioning repairman, he told me that he and his wife didn't think they could handle raising more than three kids. I assured him that my husband and I felt the same way at one point, and that before we had a change of heart, my husband Dean almost "got broken," too (the man smiled, accepting my joke).

"I know, it's truly a lot of work," I said, "but nothing worth doing is easy." I gestured toward my two boys playing nearby and said, "And these boys would not exist if we had . . ."

He nodded. "Yeah, you are so right. We would have been just like you, with eight, if we hadn't . . ."

We chatted some more and I told him how everything changes, everything is a season, as it's supposed to be. Things become easier as time goes on, I explained, and now we had four of babysitting age, and my husband and I could go out together on a whim. With multiple drivers in the family, the dynamic had changed completely. And far from being put upon, I told him all of our children begged (and openly prayed) for a new sibling.*

Of course, not everyone is called to have eight children, and in some cases there may be serious reasons to postpone pregnancy, even indefinitely. Although contraception violates the marital covenant and the natural law, God in his

---

* For those who would criticize these expectations for my older kids, first let me say they love the little ones and would do anything for them. Second, I have absolutely zero guilt about expecting every member of the family to help others when needed. I want my children to have responsibilities and to learn to care for one another, and I will never apologize for that goal.

infinite wisdom gave us ways to naturally space children, one of which is called Natural Family Planning, or NFP.

Divinely Planned Parenthood

God made the female body (and consequently the marital union) to have naturally fertile and infertile times. He also made our minds capable of discovering this cycle. Even when I was a proponent of contraception (before my reversion), I knew that there were "signs" accompanying my ovulation and fertility. NFP uses science and simple observation to determine, with great accuracy, if a woman is in a potentially fertile or infertile period of her cycle.[50]

Unlike contraception, NFP does not sterilize the marital act. It is just *information** about the way our bodies work— information we can use to decide, along with our spouse, whether to invite the possibility of new life by engaging in the marital act or to abstain from the act in order to avoid that possibility. By abstaining from the marital act (sacrificing) rather than sterilizing the marital act (insisting on pleasure alone), we show respect for the full meaning of sex as God made it.

John Paul II spoke of another benefit of using methods of family spacing like NFP:

> The choice of the natural rhythms involves accepting the cycle of the person, that is the woman, and thereby accepting dialogue, reciprocal respect, shared responsibility and self-control . . . . In this context the couple comes to experience how conjugal communion is enriched with those values of tenderness and affection

---

*   The knowledge that NFP provides is also helpful for couples trying to *achieve* pregnancy and for doctors in identifying and treating pathologies and disorders.

which constitute the inner soul of human sexuality, in its physical dimension also (FC 32).

As we teach our children about God's plan for marriage, even our little ones can begin to see the harm of contraception by first recognizing the abundant goodness of babies and children for a marriage, for a family, and for society.

REMEMBER . . .

- All Christians opposed contraception until 1930, and anti-religious, pro-Sexual-Revolution forces promoted it heavily after that.

- Contraception is wrong because it prevents the couple from becoming "one flesh" and fully giving themselves to each other through the marital act.

- NFP is different from contraception because, unlike contraception, it does not change the *nature* of the marital act and how we were made. It involves sacrificing the whole act itself, not just grasping the pleasure while ditching its natural consequences.

CONTRACEPTION

Advice for Little Kids

When our fifth child, Mark, was nine years old, he and I saw a commercial for a particular brand of "permanent birth control." A young mother, her loving husband, and their three beautiful children were in a lush, green sports field, frolicking without a care. Suddenly, the mom looked positively stricken! She walked aimlessly away from her family in a daze, while these words swam around her head onscreen:

"What if I got pregnant again?"
"What would we do?"
"*Everything* would change!"
"Will I ever stop worrying?"

Finally, Mom looked down at her youngest child who was asking her to play, and she returned to her senses. With a grand sweep of her hand, she pushed away those worries about the horror of pregnancy, finally at peace thanks to her access to "permanent birth control." The camera then cut to Mom laughing with her perfectly planned small family, elated that no more dreaded babies would show up to ruin it all.

What's Birth Control?

When I tucked Mark into bed that night, I told him how much I cherished him, because children are always a gift, never to be considered invaders against which we must "protect ourselves."

He asked me, "Mom, did you see that commercial where that mom just pushed those words away on the screen, where she was all depressed if she got pregnant, and then she was all, 'Whew! That can all go away now!'?" I told Mark I had seen it, and wasn't it so sad how they portrayed pregnancy and children?

He replied, "When I saw it, I was literally just glaring at the TV!"

In that moment, I was profoundly grateful that groups like Planned Parenthood had not tainted my sweet boy, and that he found the culture of death around him to be repulsive (thanks be to God, he still feels this way today). However, not every young child will be able to discern what is going on in a commercial or conversation about birth control. When a child asks what contraception or birth control is, you might say:

> There are some devices or pills people use so that they can't have children. Can you believe that some scientists have invented things to make sure children won't be created? It's always very bad to use these things, and isn't it sad? Some mommies and daddies even have surgery to destroy certain parts of their bodies so that those parts don't work to make children anymore.

You can explain to your little ones that a child is a beautiful gift from God, and we should always be grateful for the good gifts that God wants to give us. Remind them that

God loves all children, and that the very first command he gave to the very first married couple, Adam and Eve, was to "be fruitful and multiply"—a command that was never rescinded! In fact, the greatest gift God ever gave to us came in the form of a baby—Jesus Christ.

"HOW MANY CHILDREN DO YOU WANT?"

When people (including ourselves) reflexively say, "I only want X number of children" or "I don't want any (more) kids," we risk placing our will above God's and subtly laying the foundation for an acceptance of contraception. So when we hear our child (or even a curious adult!) ask, "How many children do you want?" the best answer may be something like this: "Well, since children are a gift from God, I would be happy with however many God wants to give us!"

This doesn't imply a mandate to have tons of kids; it simply means that you won't *reject* any child God wants to give you by willfully sterilizing the marital act through contraception or sterilization.

The Gift of a Child

A new friend of my fifth-grade son came over to play one day. When his grandmother came to pick him up, I was moved that she, a stranger, felt compelled to tell me how much this little boy had wanted and begged for a sibling. She said he was desperate for brothers—"even a foster brother!" he told his parents—as he felt so lonely at home. He had every material thing—the coolest toys, video games, and even a smart phone—and he went on trips and cruises often. But as an only child of divorced parents, the one thing his heart craved was to hang out at our house where brothers were in abundance! This desire is natural, even primal.

Dean and I used to subscribe to the culture's small-family attitude. We each have only one sibling, and when we married, we planned on having the acceptable two children, *maaaybe* stretching it to three, but no more. We used contraception, then planned on sterilization once our family was "complete." To have more, we thought, would have been irresponsible and just plain weird.

Only later, after my reversion and Dean's conversion, did it dawn on us: the notion that having many children is weird or irresponsible did not come from Christ or his Church, but from our anti-Christian culture. Having said this, I want to be very clear on a couple of things. First, we cannot judge the hearts or souls of couples who contracept (we can only judge *acts*, not souls). Second, we must not assume (unless directly told otherwise) that a couple with a small family or no children is contracepting, because infertility struggles are not uncommon. Avoid passing words of judgment or speculation about other couples—especially in front of your children.

Naysayers claim that children from big families are turned off to having many children themselves, but I have found the opposite. My children, five of whom are now adults, have always desired to have many children themselves, should God will it (and with our seven grandkids from our three married children in five years, he has been very generous in his will). Because the authentic orientation of marriage is to be openhearted in welcoming children, there is a natural draw for children to be happy with "new life" in the family and to be excited for more siblings with whom to play, grow, brawl, negotiate, mediate, and love.

If your children occasionally complain about having so many siblings (usually after a fight with one or more of them!), remind them that in the scope of their lives there will be few people who care about and love them the way their siblings will. We tell our kids that long after Dad and Mom are gone they will all have one another, which is a blessing in a grown-up world that can often be cold, cruel, and lonely.

Looking Around at Their World Today

Thanks to the Pill and other forms of contraception and sterilization, small families are the norm. Whereas in 1976 forty percent of mothers in America had at least four children, today only fourteen percent of mothers have that many.[51] We must explain to our kids that today's "norm" is actually the anomaly, and that once upon a time large families were common, normal, and celebrated.

In the seventeen years that we have lived in our current house, we've gone from raising our children alongside many other neighborhood children to being the only ones left on the street still raising little ones. We don't feel like freaks; we feel like witnesses of God's loving abundance and joy. And we want our kids to feel the same.

"DON'T YOU KNOW WHERE BABIES COME FROM?"

Neither you nor your children should apologize or be intimidated if you get flak about your family size. Living as a large family is countercultural, and your child is going to come up against those contrary voices. It may hurt, but just as Jesus didn't shout profanities at the crowds and soldiers who mocked him, we shouldn't respond with bitterness

> or anger. Instead, respond with a smile when people express surprise or even disdain about your family size. Whenever I have responded with joy, saying, "I know! Aren't they beautiful? Children are such a blessing!" most people can't help but smile and agree. And your little kids will notice.

Certainly, we all know and love people who use contraception or sterilization to limit their family size. Many of us have been there ourselves, going along with the cultural norms and expectations before we knew the truth. But God has charged each of us with the task of teaching our children well; we must not worry about our faith offending others.

Sharing the truth with your children that marriage is God's plan for bringing us children does not require judging the souls of your friends and family. You can tell your children that some people have few or no children because God hasn't gifted them with (m)any yet, but others have chosen to use pills or devices so they won't have children. Express that the latter is so sad, because they may not know how much God loves it when we accept the gift of a child from him.

By explaining it this way, you're not condemning anyone as you teach your children the truth, firmly and joyfully, as Christ commands us to do. Note well that your attitude and gentle confidence in Church teaching will set the tone for their future beliefs.

The only way to counter our culture's promotion of contraception is to be *pro-conception*, to be *for* human life. This means not just accepting the value of a baby after he is conceived, but being generously open to life to begin with, according to the way God made us.

REMEMBER ...

- A good way to explain contraception to kids is to say that it involves pills or other devices that keep mommies and daddies from having babies.

- Explain how sad it is for people to tell God through their actions that they don't want his gift of a new baby for their families. Remind them that children are always a very good thing.

- Teach your children that some people have small families or no children because God didn't gift them with many babies, and we should always pray for every family to be just the size God wills, large or small.

CONTRACEPTION
Advice for Big Kids

While I was waiting for my thirteen-year-old son who was getting a haircut, I started flipping through a women's magazine and was drawn to a slick, double-page ad for an implant contraceptive. A beautiful young woman with a radiant smile beamed out from the page with all her potential life plans laid out attractively: "get a job," "find my own place," "fall in love," "save up," "take a trip," "finish school." (Interestingly, "get married" was not among the desired options.)

The message, of course, was that women's life goals and dreams can only be achieved by using a contraceptive device. Instead of swallowing that lie, we should ask this question: "What's so wrong with women's bodies, anyway?"

If It Ain't Broke . . .

Today's teens have been born and bred to have "green" sensibilities, wanting to embrace foods, products, and lifestyles that are seen as natural and healthy. There is nothing inherently wrong with this mindset, and it can even help young people understand why contraception is a literal pollution to our healthy bodies, a distortion of God's plan and how he made us, and an affront to women's dignity.

Contraception rests on the presumption that there is something wrong or incomplete about a woman's body. She is usually the one expected to bear the "responsibility" of contraception. The woman (or not-fully-grown girl) is the one expected to put powerful steroids (the Pill) into her body, have hormonal implants inserted under her skin, or have "pediatrician-approved" IUDs—plastic and metal foreign objects—forcibly inserted into her uterus. All in order to become a sterile sexual object for men.

The picture of glorious "health" projected by the slick ad I viewed in the magazine can only be believed if you ignore the long list of "common side effects," including (but not limited to):

- Mood swings/nervousness/depressed mood
- Weight gain
- Headache
- Acne
- Nausea/stomach pain
- Vaginitis (inflammation of the vagina) and breast pain

Add to that the risks that the girl or woman must take on, including (but not limited to):

- Ectopic pregnancy
- Ovarian cysts
- Possibly fatal blood clots resulting in stroke/heart attack/ DVT/embolism/blindness
- Migration of implant to a blood vessel in lung
- High blood pressure

- Liver tumors
- Breast cancer

But hey, those risks must be worth it, because without these implants and chemicals, how could a woman *ever* travel or get her own place? I'm being sarcastic of course, but that's the lie our daughters are being sold.

Trent shared with me a heartbreaking story of a co-worker who used an intrauterine device (IUD) and developed Pelvic Inflammatory Disease (PID). She mournfully told him, "I didn't want a baby, but now I'm on permanent birth control"—because the PID rendered her infertile.

A well-formed Catholic teen should look at this evidence and conclude that there is something wrong with this twisted view of women's bodies, *not* with the way God made them. The physical dangers of contraception (not to mention the spiritual danger!) should also give pause to any parent who thinks a daughter should be on birth control "just in case."

Not much could be more shaming and degrading to a teen girl than to make her think there is something wrong with the way she is made, and that her "full potential" cannot be achieved unless her female body mimics a man's inability to get pregnant. Beware of any message that tells our daughters it's somehow unfair or unfortunate that they were created female.

Is NFP a Form of Contraception?

When you teach your teen that contraception is immoral but Natural Family Planning is licit, he may ask, "But Mom, isn't NFP just another form of contraception? I mean, in both cases you're trying not to have a baby." In response, tell your teen that we must distinguish between the *means* and the *ends*. Just because our intended *end* is morally allowed (in this case, avoiding pregnancy), it does not follow that any old means we use to get there is automatically moral, too.

For example, imagine two women, Mary and Sarah, both of whom want to lose weight. Mary chooses to eat a healthy diet, limit portions, and occasionally fast, whereas Sarah just throws up her food after eating. Even though they have the same goal or *end* (losing weight), Sarah's way or *means* of achieving that goal (self-induced vomiting) is disordered and unhealthy.

Just as bulimia contradicts the body's design by seeking the *pleasure* of eating while thwarting its life-giving *purpose*, contraception contradicts the body's design by seeking the *pleasure* of sex while willfully thwarting its life-giving *purpose*. By contrast, sacrificing sex to avoid a pregnancy (like sacrificing eating to avoid calories) is not thwarting or disordering the nature of the sex act, since there is no act at all. We can teach our teens the truth that contraception is essentially "sexual bulimia."

Another helpful analogy used to explain NFP compares the marital act to the act of sending a wedding invitation. When a couple has sex during the fertile period, that's like sending a wedding invitation to a relative who is likely able to attend the wedding. In both cases there's a good chance that a wonderful person will show up a few months later. When a couple has sex during the infertile period, that's like sending a wedding invitation to a relative who is probably not able to attend the wedding. The person isn't expected to show up, but if he does, he will be welcomed.

By contrast, when a couple uses contraception, that's like sending a "dis-invitation"—an announcement that says, "Don't come to our wedding; you're not wanted here!" Using contraception sends the message to your future child (as well as to God, who is responsible for every blessing of pregnancy), "We want sexual pleasure *at this specific time when you would be conceived*, but you'd better not show up and ruin it!"

The truth is, children don't ruin sexual pleasure; they are its fulfillment. Help your teen to understand that we should never engage in the baby-making act while simultaneously sending the message that a baby is unwanted. The Lord asks us to live with *integrity*, in our bodies as well as our souls.

KEEPING OUR VOWS

When Catholics marry, they vow always to be faithful to one another and to be open to life. "But," some people ask, "can't I keep my vow to be open to life by only occasionally using contraception?" That's like saying, "Can't I keep my vow to be faithful by only having an affair every now and then?" A couple's promises to be faithful and to lovingly welcome children from God are not reserved just for *some* sexual acts, but for *every marital act* between husband and wife—because sex between a husband and wife is a renewal of every vow we made at our wedding.

What About Overpopulation?

In 2012, when Melinda Gates pledged to donate $4.6 billion to promote contraception in Africa in order to fight "overpopulation," my friend Obianuju Ekeocha wrote an open letter to Gates that caused quite a stir. As someone who grew up in rural Africa, Uju (as her friends call her) explained that this money would be better spent on health care, food, and education. She said, "I see this $4.6 billion buying us misery. I see it buying us unfaithful husbands. I see it buying us streets devoid of the innocent chatter of children. I see it buying us disease and untimely death."[52]

Stephan Karanja, the former secretary-general of the Kenyan Medical Association, has said: "Our health sector is collapsed. Thousands of the Kenyan people will die of malaria, the treatment for which costs a few cents, in health facilities whose shelves are stocked to the ceiling with millions of dollars' worth of pills, IUDs, Norplant, Depo-Provera, and so on, most of which are supplied with American money."[53]

The truth is that overpopulation is a myth. Explain to your teen that the earth is not overflowing with people. Every person living today could fit in the state of Texas with room to spare, leaving the rest of North America and all the other continents uninhabited (do the math).[54] A planet that is almost completely uninhabited hardly screams "no more room!" There is enough food on the planet to feed everyone; we just don't use resources effectively.[55] God does not fail to provide for his children, so why do people go hungry? We can lay the blame at the feet of sinful man. For example, Africa is a continent rich with natural resources, but also replete with corrupt governments, greedy officials, evil warlords, and countless wars. It is human sin and failure, not a lack of food or resources, that is the enemy here.

BIRTH CONTROL FOR HEALTH REASONS?

Quite often, doctors will advise teenage girls to use hormonal contraception to treat problems like menstrual disorders. Although using hormones for this reason does not constitute the sin of contracepting, it tends only to alleviate symptoms rather than fix the underlying pathology.

Doctors routinely prescribe the Pill for "female problems" because that's how they are taught in medical school to treat such issues; it's the only tool in their toolbox, so to speak. Also, many doctors believe that girls should be on contraception anyway, in case they become sexually active.

Aside from myriad health risks for your daughter, such as weight gain, headaches, blood clots, and strokes, taking the Pill might convince her she "can't get pregnant," making it more likely she'll say "yes" if pressured to have sex. Your best bet is to consult a faithful, Catholic pediatrician or family doctor (NaPro-trained, for example) who can almost always recommend safer and more effective alternatives.[56]

Birth Control to Prevent Abortion?

If your teen is pro-life, or is at least ambivalent about abortion (which most people are), then he may be sympathetic to the idea that we can reduce abortions by promoting contraception. But it's a flawed belief.

On one university campus, a group of students chastised Trent for not passing out condoms during a pro-life outreach. He told them he didn't have to, because the campus health center gave away condoms for free. One man responded, "But the center is all the way on the other side of campus. I don't want to have to walk all the way over there just for condoms. You guys should be passing them out here."

Now, if this young man was too lazy to walk a few hundred yards for condoms, why in the world would we expect him to work hard to provide for a child should the condom fail and his partner become pregnant? The words of John Paul II from *Evangelium Vitae* (EV) apply here:

> It may be that many people use contraception with a view to excluding the subsequent temptation of abortion. But the negative values inherent in the "contraceptive mentality"—which is very different from responsible parenthood, lived in respect for the full truth of the conjugal act—are such that they in fact *strengthen this temptation when an unwanted life is conceived* [emphasis added] (13).

The saint is right. If a child is conceived in spite of a couple's attempt to stop him from coming into existence through contraception, then it is much more likely that child will lose his life through abortion. Even Planned Parenthood's research shows that more than half of women who come in for abortions were using contraception during the month they got pregnant.[57]

Contraception and abortion are also historically linked. *Roe v. Wade*, the 1973 Supreme Court decision that legalized abortion, was based on a so-called "right to privacy" that first appeared in *Griswold v. Connecticut* (1965)—which legalized the sale of contraceptives! And not only did contraception pave the way for abortion legally, it now *keeps* abortion legal, philosophically. In *Planned Parenthood v. Casey* (1992), the Supreme Court said that women's societal equality depends on "the availability of abortion in the event that contraception should fail."

Contraception *requires* abortion as a back-up!

When the pro-abortion members of the Supreme Court *and* the Catholic Church both see the same truth, we should take note. Contraception and abortion are symbiotically connected, and a society's supporting the first inevitably leads to its supporting the second. The anti-life attitudes fueled by contraception will become even more obvious as we discuss what the Church teaches about abortion.

REMEMBER...

- Tell your teens that contraception disrespects women and their bodies by expecting them to endure serious risks and side effects just so they can be like men in their inability to become pregnant.

- Poverty in developing nations should be addressed by promoting health, development, and education, not by pushing contraceptives to decrease a nation's children.

- Teens who are against abortion should be shown the many ways in which contraception and abortion are linked. In the words of John Paul II, "contraception and abortion are often closely connected, as fruits of the same tree."[58]

7

ABORTION
What the Church Teaches

Sometimes elements of our culture go so far over the edge that they unintentionally reveal a truth many people want to deny. Consider what Peter Singer, a world-renowned moral philosopher at Princeton University, says about the value of a *newborn* baby:

> The fact that a being is a human being, in the sense of a member of the species *homo sapiens*, is not relevant to the wrongness of killing it; it is, rather, characteristics like rationality, autonomy, and self-consciousness that make a difference. Infants lack these characteristics. Killing them, therefore, cannot be equated with killing normal human beings, or any other self-conscious beings . . . . The main point is clear: killing a disabled infant is not morally equivalent to killing a person. Very often it is not wrong at all.[59]

Some pretty sick stuff, right?

Keep in mind, though, that Singer's philosophical argument for infanticide isn't just one person's crazy opinion. In

2012, a completely earnest article defending what the authors call "after-birth abortion" was published in the prestigious *Journal of Medical Ethics*.[60]

But in the midst of this evil talk, there exists in Singer's philosophy a thread of honesty and truth. He writes:

> The pro-life groups were right about one thing, the location of the baby inside or outside the womb cannot make much of a moral difference. We cannot coherently hold it is all right to kill a fetus a week before birth, but as soon as the baby is born everything must be done to keep it alive.

Although he gets that part right, his chilling solution to the abortion debate is "not to accept the pro-life view that the fetus is a human being with the same moral status as yours or mine. The solution is the very opposite, to abandon the idea that all human life is of equal worth."[61] In other words, instead of cherishing unborn babies as we do newborn babies, we should be permitted to kill newborn babies just as we are permitted to kill unborn babies!

This philosophy is a clear example of the *culture of death* that Pope St. John Paul II warned us about and another reason we should be grateful that the Catholic Church stands, unwaveringly, on the side of life.

What Faith Tells Us

The earliest Christian reference to abortion can be found in a first-century text called the *Didache*, which states, "You shall not procure abortion, nor destroy a newborn child" (2:1–2). According to the *Catechism*, "Since the first century the Church has affirmed the moral evil of every procured abortion. This teaching has not changed and remains unchangeable. Direct abortion, that is to say, abortion willed either as an end or a means, is gravely contrary to the moral law" (2271).

A UNIVERSAL TEACHING

"Throughout Christianity's 2,000-year history, this same doctrine has been constantly taught by the Fathers of the Church and by her pastors and Doctors. Even scientific and philosophical discussions about the precise moment of the infusion of the spiritual soul have never given rise to any hesitation about the moral condemnation of abortion" (EV 61).

Christians always knew that the act of abortion was wrong even when they weren't sure exactly, as a matter of biology, when human life began. This evidence is powerfully articulated by St. Basil the Great, who wrote in the fourth century, "The woman who purposely destroys her unborn child is guilty of murder. With us there is no nice enquiry as to its being formed or unformed."[62] And even though the Bible never explicitly mentions abortion, what it teaches about respecting human life applies to *all* human life—including life in the womb.

God forbids the murder of human beings (Exod. 20:13, Prov. 6:16–17) because human beings are made in his image (Gen. 1:26–27), even from the first moment of their existence. The CDF instruction *Dignitatis Personae* (DP) declares, "The body of a human being, from the very first stages of its existence, can never be reduced merely to a group of cells . . . . The human being is to be respected and treated as a person from the moment of conception" (4).

The modern biological facts about human development, as well as the Church's universal condemnation of abortion, led John Paul II to teach authoritatively:

> I declare that direct abortion, that is, abortion willed as an end or as a means, always constitutes a grave moral disorder, since it is the deliberate killing of an innocent human being. This doctrine is based upon the natural law and upon the written word of God, is transmitted by the Church's Tradition and taught by the ordinary and universal Magisterium (EV 62).

In other words, the Church's teaching on the intrinsic evil of abortion can never and will never change.

What Reason Tells Us

You don't have to be Catholic or even religious to know that a new human life begins at conception and thus that abortion is wrong. The science of embryology long ago recognized that at conception (the fertilization of the egg by a sperm cell) a new and distinct human being comes into existence. When I was homeschooling my daughter during her sixth grade year, her secular science book began its chapter on human biology with the following sentence: "You began life as a single cell."

The words *embryo* (a Greek word that means "young one") and *fetus* (a Latin word that means "offspring") refer to stages of development in the life of a human being. If a fetus or unborn child is growing, then he or she must be alive. If an unborn child has human parents and human DNA, then he or she must be human.

An unborn child is not a body *part* like skin cells or sperm or egg. Instead, he or she is an *organism*: a whole, intact individual being who, like the rest of us, will grow and develop with time, nutrients, and the right environment. The unborn child is at the exact size and location he or she is *supposed* to be at that particular stage of human development. We've all been through the same course of development in our own lives, no exceptions. Every one of us was *conceived* (our beginning!) and grew through our proper stages as a human being.

The logic is clear: if it is wrong to directly kill an innocent human being, and if an unborn child is an innocent human being, then abortion is wrong because it directly, indeed *violently*, kills an innocent human being.

CITE THE EXPERTS

The standard medical text *Human Embryology and Teratology* states that "fertilization [also called conception] is a critical landmark because, under ordinary circumstances, a new, genetically distinct human organism is formed."[63] Even David Boonin, who wrote *A Defense of Abortion* and publicly debated Trent on this issue, admits, "Perhaps the most straightforward relation between you and me on the one hand and every human fetus on the other is this: all are living members of the same species, *homo sapiens*. A human fetus, after all, is simply a human being at a very early stage in his or her development."[64]

Building a Culture of Life

The Church's teaching on abortion could not be clearer, and we all know this truth ("it is wrong to directly kill an innocent human being") in our hearts—even though some people try very hard to deny it. John Paul II spoke of abortion in terms of the natural law: "No circumstance, no purpose, no law whatsoever can ever make licit an act which is intrinsically illicit, since it is contrary to the law of God which is written in every human heart, knowable by reason itself, and proclaimed by the Church" (EV 62).

Abortion has been sold to us as a solution to our problems, but there are millions of women (and men) who have been wounded and even devastated by it. Their healing will not come from ignoring this issue but instead from a clear affirmation of God's love in spite of our sins, including the sin of abortion. For those who have been involved with an abortion procedure, please hear these beautiful words from John Paul II:

> Do not give in to discouragement and do not lose hope. Try rather to understand what happened and face it honestly. If you have not already done so, give yourselves over with humility and trust to repentance. The Father of mercies is ready to give you his forgiveness and his peace in the sacrament of reconciliation. To the same Father and his mercy you can with sure hope entrust your child. With the friendly and expert help and advice of other people, and as a result of your own painful experience, you can be among the most eloquent defenders of everyone's right to life.[65]

When we choose to target and kill an innocent human being as an answer to our problems, we fail to love. In order to love our neighbor, including our newly conceived neighbors, we must work to build a culture of life in the hearts and minds of our children, so that we, as a society, may come to view abortion as unthinkable.

REMEMBER...

- The Church has consistently taught that abortion is an intrinsic moral evil.

- We can know from reason that the unborn, from the moment of conception, are human beings, and that killing them through abortion is wrong.

- Those who have procured abortions can find healing and forgiveness from God, and, through his grace, become eloquent defenders of human life.

ABORTION

Advice for Little Kids

After her children had gone to sleep one night, pro-life author Jean Garton was finishing work on a presentation on abortion that included a picture of a baby aborted at ten weeks. She narrates what happened next:

> Suddenly I heard, rather than saw, another person near me. At the sound of a sharp intake of breath, I turned to find that my youngest son, then a sleepy, rumpled three-year-old, had unexpectedly and silently entered the room. His small voice was filled with great sadness as he asked, "Who broke the baby?"[66]

Explaining abortion to a young child is an awful, horrifying thing to do. In our home, this explanation is necessary because of our involvement with crisis pregnancy centers and diocesan pro-life activities. Our kids start to hear the word "abortion" at a fairly young age, and so at a certain point I must tell them, gently, the meaning of the word.

PICTURES OF ABORTION

When should a child be allowed to see photos of aborted children? It's up to the parents to decide when their child is emotionally mature enough to see those images. Personally, I stumbled upon graphic photos in a booklet when I was about ten years old, and seeing the ugly truth of abortion cemented my pro-life beliefs from that day on. No matter what you choose for your own small children, after kids hit puberty and have the physical ability to make a baby, they should be ready to see what happens in an abortion.

Explaining the Unthinkable

It's dreadfully surreal when a *mother* first exposes the concept of abortion to her child. I usually take a deep breath and say, "Sometimes mommies or daddies don't want their babies, and they pay a doctor to take the baby out too soon." Obviously, this is simplistic and not the full range of scenarios, but it leads to the next question: "But what happens to the baby?" Your honest answer: "It's very sad, honey, but the baby dies."

So far, each of my children has had the same reaction: disbelief, confusion, denial, and alarm. "How could anyone do that?" they ask, recoiling. "Who forces a mommy to do that?" "Why would a doctor do that to a little baby?"

Children are naturally pro-life, and they really get the horror of it.

You don't have to paint a picture or get graphic. The idea of someone deliberately killing a baby in his mother's womb is so foreign to small children as to be absurd, nonsensical, insane. Their little minds sense the disorder and evil immediately, and they reject it.

After our little ones experience that initial shock, we

must be sure to remind them about God's mercy and about our duty to love both the babies and their mothers. You might say something like this:

> I know! It's so sad that someone would do this. Some mommies think they can't take care of the baby and others don't even think it *is* a baby, because people have lied to them about that. But lots of mommies feel terrible later, because deep down they know that what they did was wrong. But God loves us and he always wants to help us, even if we do something really bad. So let's pray for the mommies, daddies, and doctors who do this, because God and those little babies want to see all of them in heaven one day.[67]

MOURNING MISCARRIAGE

Sometimes children learn of the value of human life when their mother has a miscarriage. When I miscarried our seventh child, our children were heartbroken. They had anticipated and already loved this little one as their sibling! We allowed them to mourn, to write poems, and to draw pictures for the child we lost. We have those memorials to this day, tucked away. None of them, even those in adulthood now, have forgotten that sibling. They hope in an eternal meeting one day. What a beautiful lesson for children about the inherent worth of each and every human life!

A Light in the Darkness

When we explain abortion to children, it can feel like we're taking away their innocence. After all, once they understand that our nation not only allows but celebrates the murder of children nestled in their mothers' wombs, just as they or their siblings had been nestled so recently, how could they not be affected to their core? But it's important to balance the darkness of abortion with the light of God's truth. Here are three concepts that refute the pro-abortion mindset (and many other evils), which you can and should instill in even your smallest children:

- **The Beauty of Human Life:** This is the easiest (and most fun) way to teach your children to be pro-life. There are lots of great videos on the internet that show human development in the womb through 4D ultrasound, computer graphics, and even high definition videos shot from inside the uterus with a tiny camera.[68] Another fun thing is to borrow a fetal model display from a pro-life organization and let your children hold and love these tiny model babies. And here is a "guessing game" that will delight your children and stick with them forever: pull out the children's Bible and have them tell you how many people were at the Visitation (Luke 1:39-44). They may guess two at first, but then they will see that there were four: Mary, Elizabeth, Jesus, and John!

- **The Equal Dignity of Human Beings:** I remember reading a pro-life author who described what happened when his seven-year-old saw a double amputee. She whispered to her father that the man had no legs, but then she said to him, drawing on the lessons he taught her, "But he is still just as valuable as everyone else!" Teach your children early that our dignity and value as human beings is *the same* no matter how smart, strong, or old we are—or aren't. And of course, as they say in that children's classic, *Horton Hears a Who*: "A person's a person, no matter how small."

- **Good Ends Don't Justify Evil Means:** The most basic principle of the natural law and Christian morality is, "Do good, avoid evil." Unfortunately, some people think that it's okay to do "what is necessary" to achieve a good end, even if the means of getting there are evil. Always remind your children that, if they have a problem, they must never do something wrong—even a little wrong—in order to solve it. For example, a kid can't cheat "just a little" on a test in order to get a good grade and make Dad proud, just as Dad can't secretly skip out on his work behind his boss's back to spend time with his family.

Finally, explain to your children that many people *have* changed their hearts on the issue of abortion, including women and men who have procured them and even abortionists themselves! Some of them even fight against abortion similar to the way that St. Paul, who used to murder Christians, went on to become one of the greatest Christians of all time. Let them know that even though the world can be an unfair and even scary place, God is bigger than the world because he created it. Jesus said, "In the world you will have trouble; but don't be afraid, I have overcome the world!" (John 16:33).

REMEMBER...

- If small children need to learn what the word "abortion" means, explain in a calm, clear way, with sadness, but without unnecessary graphic elements.

- Children are naturally pro-life and so will naturally recoil when learning about abortion.

- Teach your children moral truths that will undergird their pro-life beliefs as they get older, such as, "All humans are equal," and "Good ends don't justify evil means."

ABORTION

Advice for Big Kids

The world can do a number on naturally pro-life children once they reach puberty. Peer pressure, appeals to emotion, and fuzzy reasoning to justify an escape from an unintended pregnancy can obscure the simple truth that a pregnant woman has a baby inside her and that baby shouldn't be killed.

Our job as parents is to help our kids see past the lies that bombard them from every side and give them the tools they need to make "a case for life."

The SLED Test

People who defend legal abortion often admit that the unborn are technically "human" but claim they are not "persons." Conveniently, their definition of a "person" is vague—including just enough detail to disqualify the unborn. These nebulous arguments can be seductive and are popular with high school and college students who identify as "pro-choice." However, one of the best answers to these arguments (which came to me in the form of an internet comment that hit me like a ton of bricks) goes like this:

"We only question the personhood of someone we wish to harm."

Feel the weight of that truth, and test it. Try to think of a time when a human being's personhood was questioned for a motive *other than* using, marginalizing, harming, or killing him. From American slavery to the Nazi holocaust, the *whole point* of questioning the personhood of others is to deny them human rights. It's a rhetorical (and arbitrary) technique used to *exclude* rather than include human beings. This should resonate with your teen, whose generation has been inculcated in the value of "inclusion."

We must focus on the natural-law principles that forbid killing innocent human beings or treating them as if they weren't really human, and we must share the simple truth that all human beings are persons, no exceptions.

The existence of atheists who oppose abortion and of secular pro-life organizations prove that being against abortion is not merely a religious issue.[69] Abortion is a *human rights* issue. Stephen Schwartz is a philosopher who shows, through non-religious reasoning, that none of these differences between born and unborn humans deprives any human being of basic rights. He summarizes his argument with the acronym SLED:[70]

- **S – Size:** A baby in the womb might be tiny, but how big do you have to be to be a person? And who decides? A baby in the womb is the exact size he is supposed to be for his age. A person's intrinsic dignity should never be determined by his size.

- **L – Level of Development:** Unborn babies can't think like you or I do, but neither can newborn babies or some adults with disabilities. Feeling pain or perceiving experiences (what is called "sentience") also doesn't make us human persons; after all, rats and pigeons are sentient. Our value and our human rights come not from what we can *do*, but simply from what we *are*: human beings.

- **E – Environment:** A baby in the womb isn't born yet, but so what? Our location cannot change our value or who we are. Remember what abortion and infanticide advocate Peter Singer said: "the location of the baby inside or outside the womb cannot make much of a moral difference."

- **D – Degree of Dependency:** You'll hear it said, "It can't live without the mother!" But that's an argument *against* abortion! It makes no sense that we consider it despicable to abandon a *newborn* baby who cannot live without total dependence on another, but justifiable to kill an *unborn* baby who cannot live without total dependence on another. A civilized society *protects* those who are weaker and more vulnerable; we don't authorize their killings.

Pro-lifers, please don't be fooled or intimidated. The abortion advocates' murky philosophical discussion of "personhood" is not a noble or nuanced search for what is true about the human person. It's simply an excuse for one group of humans to dehumanize, oppress, and kill another group of humans. When you or your teen is faced with these arguments, simply ask, "Why does the difference between born and unborn humans matter? Shouldn't we protect all human beings no matter how different they are from us?"

> **"I'M PREGNANT AND SCARED."**
> When a teen becomes pregnant, whether it's your own child or your child's friend, those around her

should meet her where she is, reaching out with great love and mercy. Help her see a way forward that does not include abortion. Encourage a visit to a trusted pro-life doctor or pregnancy resource center, and don't be afraid to enlist others in the Catholic community for support. If she is still tempted by the "easy solution" promised by abortion advocates, you'll want to share with her the testimonies of women who believed the lie of the "quick fix" and whose abortions still haunt them years or decades later (a good website for these stories is silentnomoreawareness.org).

Tougher Questions

As your children enter middle school, high school, and college, they will be bombarded with "pro-choice" arguments that try to obscure the real issue: are unborn children human beings, and what does abortion do to them? I highly recommend Trent's book, *Persuasive Pro-Life*, for the complete refutation of these arguments, but for now, here are some quick responses for your teens:

- **"If we make abortion illegal, then women will just get dangerous 'back-alley abortions.'"** We don't make it legal for big people to kill little people so that it's safer for the big people to kill little people. Besides, in countries where almost all abortions have been illegal, like Ireland (until recently) and Poland, maternal mortality (the rate at which pregnant women die) is lower than in the United States, which shows that abortion isn't necessary to protect women's health.[71]

- **"If you're pro-life, then why aren't you a vegetarian who is against all wars?"** Pro-life doesn't mean it's wrong to kill any life (it's okay to use antibiotics or eat hamburgers), and it doesn't even mean it's wrong to kill human life (even your pacifist friends will likely agree that a woman being attacked by a serial killer may shoot him in self-defense). Even war may be necessary and morally licit in some cases to protect human life from aggressors. But just as we may never directly target and kill innocent human beings within a war zone, for example, we may never directly target and kill babies in the womb. The real question is why more people who protest wars or factory farming don't also protest the dismemberment of unborn human children through abortion!

- **"Even if it is a baby, it's still my body, my choice."** At least this argument doesn't try to make the case that a fetus is a literal "part of the woman's body" (which is absurd, as no woman's body has an extra head, eight limbs, and, half the time, a penis). But it does distort the relationship between mother and child in order to justify abortion. Just because you have power over someone does not give you the right to hurt that person. In early America, the law said that a slave's body belonged to the slaveowner. Should we continue to let the powerful oppress the weak simply because they can? If you don't want a baby, don't engage in the baby-making act. If you go ahead and engage in that act, be prepared to take responsibility for any baby you create, as decency, responsibility, and maturity demand.

The Hard Cases

Teens are often susceptible to emotion-based arguments, such as those that appeal to "hard cases" like rape or danger to a woman's life. But we must get them to understand that abortion is an *intrinsically* evil act, which means it is evil *by its very nature*, and no circumstance can ever make it moral or good.

Ask them: if we permit the grave evil of killing unborn babies under some circumstances, how can we say that any other evil is "off limits" in the name of some hard case or greater good? There's not a petty thief or genocidal dictator who didn't think he was acting for a perceived greater good, after all. The natural moral law exists to keep us grounded—especially when we encounter those hard cases when our emotions would take us elsewhere.

Space does not permit us to address every aspect of these cases, but for the purposes of teaching your teens, here are the main points you should address:

- **The Life of the Mother:** Numerous doctors and health care professionals attest that there is never an illness or condition that requires direct abortion as a cure. Sometimes doctors will foresee that an unborn child might die during a medical intervention that is used to save the mother's life, but the death of the child is neither the goal nor the means of the treatment. For example, it is moral to use radiation to kill cancer cells in a pregnant woman's body even if the radiation inadvertently kills her unborn child. The loss of the child is an *unintended side effect* of a moral medical treatment, and if the child came through unharmed, everyone would rejoice! But it is always wrong to engage in an act where an innocent person is *directly targeted and killed* whether as an end or as the means to an end.[72]

- **Pregnancies Due to Rape:** We should do everything we can to help this child's mother and bring the rapist to swift justice. She is an innocent victim who should not be blamed or punished for what happened to her. But her child is also innocent and should not be punished for what his or her father has done. The woman needs healing from the trauma of rape, but this healing will not be helped by the additional violence and trauma that comes with ending her child's life.[73] It is never just to kill innocent members of our human family, even in an attempt to right an egregious wrong. Love is always the right response, and taking an innocent life is never an act of love.

Real Social Justice

When you explain abortion to teens, appeal to their sense of honor, heroism, and maturity. It's fashionable for teens to take up the cause of "social justice," wanting to fight for those who are weak and vulnerable. Remind them that, to be consistent, they must be pro-life on abortion, as it is *always* wrong for bigger and stronger groups of people to marginalize and kill smaller and weaker groups of people.

The strong killing the weak is the classic "oppression model," and there is no class of human beings on the planet more vulnerable, voiceless, defenseless, marginalized, and dehumanized than the unborn. Any cry of "Abortion liberates women!" is undermined by the truth that abortion turns the "oppressed" (women) into the oppressor. Pushing oppression down the line, as any warrior for justice can see, is not the solution for ending oppression.

Your children should know that our all-powerful and ever-loving Father does not give us a cross without the means to carry it through to glorious redemption. We must trust him, knowing that every human life is sacred, even in the hard cases. Let us rejoice that our task of raising pro-life children grows easier as we see more and more young people identifying as pro-life, willing to fight for and protect the tiniest members of our human family.

REMEMBER...

- A basic principle of the natural law is that we may never deliberately kill innocent human beings, even if we think others might benefit from their deaths.

- Arguments against "personhood" are only put forth by those who wish to harm certain other human beings. Denying "personhood" (and thus human rights) based on arbitrary criteria such as size, location, or dependency (unborn humans) is as wrong as denying them based on skin color (black humans) or ethnicity (Jewish humans).

- The hard cases don't justify abortion because we are never permitted to commit an evil, even in order to answer another evil or prevent suffering.

8

REPRODUCTIVE TECHNOLOGIES

What the Church Teaches

Many years ago, I was teaching an introductory faith-formation class at my parish, and during one of my presentations I spoke about in-vitro fertilization (IVF), the process by which children are conceived in a laboratory vessel using procured eggs and sperm. A woman approached me afterward, revealing that both she and her sister had struggled with infertility and that her sister had resorted to using IVF.

"I tried to convince my sister not to do it, that it was against God's law and Church teaching, but I didn't have the right words," she told me. "I'm so happy you're teaching about this!"

In my excitement and pride, I basked in the "I-taught-a-good-class" afterglow—until I heard what she said next:

"Even though I also had infertility issues, my husband and I never considered IVF. We used artificial insemination to conceive our daughter. She is such a blessing! I am so grateful that we were able to conceive her in a way that didn't go against our faith."

I was taken aback, so I sent up a quick prayer to the Holy Spirit before I said to her in a softened voice, "Oh . . . I am so sorry to tell you this, but it is also wrong to conceive a child using artificial insemination."

In an instant, the joy went out of her face, and she became very quiet. The woman was very gracious, but I could tell that her mind was now troubled and that she wanted to be somewhere else. She thanked me again and quickly left the class.

It can be hard to share Catholic teaching on assisted reproductive technology (ART) because on the surface it seems "pro-life." People who are skeptical of Church teaching may say, "I understand why Catholics are against abortion because that kills a baby, but what's wrong with technology that helps *make* a baby?"

PRAISE FOR *MORAL* INFERTILITY TREATMENT

The Catholic Church recognizes what a blessing it is when science *ethically* helps a couple recover their own ability to conceive a child. The *Catechism* says, "Couples who discover that they are sterile suffer greatly . . . . Research aimed at reducing human sterility is to be encouraged, on condition that it is placed at the service of the human person, of his inalienable rights, and his true and integral good according to the design and will of God" (2375).

Assisting but Not Replacing

In 2008, the Congregation for the Doctrine of Faith released *Dignitatis Personae*, which addresses questions related to the treatment of infertility and the generation of human life. It laid down a clear principle: fertility treatments that "substitute for the conjugal act" are not permitted, but those that "act *as an aid to the conjugal act and its fertility*" are permitted (12).

In other words, when evaluating a fertility treatment, we should ask this question: *Does the treatment help a husband and wife have sex and conceive a child from that union, or does it replace the sexual act with something else?*

Medicines that stimulate egg and sperm production, as well as surgeries that unblock fallopian tubes, treat endometriosis, repair the function of the penis, etc., are examples of *moral* treatments, because they *facilitate* rather than *replace* the marital act and natural conception (DP 13). These interventions order and heal the body to make sure it functions properly.

Unfortunately, many other popular techniques for dealing with infertility are *immoral*, because they violate the principle that a human being must, in the words of the CDF instruction *Donum Vitae* (DV), "be brought about as the fruit of the conjugal act specific to the love between spouses" (4). The *Catechism* says:

> Techniques that entail the dissociation of husband and wife, by the intrusion of a person other than the couple (donation of sperm or ovum, surrogate uterus), are gravely immoral. These techniques (heterologous artificial insemination and fertilization) infringe the child's right to be born of a father and mother known to him and bound to each other by marriage. They betray the spouses' "right to become a father and a mother only through each other" (2376).

The dignity of the human person "demands" that children should come into existence from the love that exists between a mother and father. A child should not be the end result of a financial transaction among any combination of men, women, egg, or sperm donors, and/or "surrogates" who rent out their wombs.

Please note! A child conceived from immoral techniques is still a precious human being made in God's image, possessing intrinsic dignity and full human rights. But the profound goodness of this child's existence does not justify the sinful *means* that brought him into being—just as a child conceived from a one-night stand or even a rape deserves our full love, respect, and care, even though the circumstances of his conception contradicted God's law.

In our discussion of contraception we saw how sex becomes distorted when it seeks the union of the couple without being open to life. But the sacredness of the marital act also prohibits any means of procreation that seek the good of being "open to life" *without* the union of the couple. A child has the natural right "to be born of a father and mother known to him and bound to each other by marriage." We adults tend to think of our "right" to a child, but the Church is clear that a child "is not something owed to one, but is a gift . . . . A child may not be considered a piece of property, an idea to which an alleged 'right to a child' would lead. In this area, only the child possesses genuine rights" (CCC 2378).

Immoral reproductive technologies abandon this principle and turn a child into a *product* or commodity that is manufactured for the good of those who purchased him, which always violates the child's dignity.

WHAT ABOUT ARTIFICIAL INSEMINATION?

In the next chapters we will see the damage that happens when children are brought into existence through "donor" sperm and eggs (*heterologous artificial insemination*). But even *homologous* artificial insemination—

which involves only the sperm and egg of the husband and wife—is wrong when it replaces the marital act with a medical procedure (CCC 2377).*

In-Vitro Fertilization (IVF)

Years ago, I was listening to Ron Reagan Jr. advocate on television for embryonic stem cell research. He was strongly in support of using "excess" human embryos from IVF labs for research material. He caught my full attention when he dismissed pro-lifers' objections to human embryo research by noting with a smug chuckle: "Look, if pro-life Christians were *really* interested in the protection of human embryos, if they *really* thought those embryos were babies, they'd be against IVF as well."

Ron thought he was making a clever point, and he was—he just didn't realize the Catholic Church had been making that same point for years: if you care about unborn human life, you must protect it from both the abortionist and the IVF doctor.

Unlike the marital act, IVF creates embryos *outside* of the woman's body in a clinic or laboratory. Healthy embryos are later implanted in a woman's womb, while unhealthy or even healthy but unwanted embryonic human beings are destroyed. *Dignitatis Personae* points out that "in any other area of medicine, ordinary professional ethics and the healthcare authorities themselves would never allow a medical procedure which involved such a high number of failures and fatalities" (15).

---

* Furthermore, with both kinds of artificial insemination, sperm is typically collected through the intrinsically immoral act of masturbation. Some Catholic moral theologians, however, consider the practice of *Gamete Intrafallopian Transfer* (GIFT)—in which sperm and egg are introduced to the woman's fallopian tubes for fertilization to occur—to be morally licit if the sperm are collected via the natural, completed marital act.

But even if IVF were performed without destroying "excess" embryos, it would still be wrong, because it separates what God himself has joined: the unitive and procreative aspects of the marital act. In the process, children are commodified and exploited, as the CDF explains:

> Such fertilization entrusts the life and identity of the embryo into the power of doctors and biologists and establishes the domination of technology over the origin and destiny of the human person. Such a relationship of domination is in itself contrary to the dignity and equality that must be common to parents and children (DP 17).

Unexpected Blessings

Remember the woman who left my class upset at what I had told her about artificial insemination? I wanted to better explain the Church's teaching at the following week's class, but, although she had been a regular, she never came back. We never spoke again. For a while, I worried that my decision to tell her the truth might have caused her to leave the Church.

Fast forward about a year or two.

I was reading our diocesan newspaper when I saw a feature story about Catholics who had undergone immoral reproductive treatments but who now embrace Church teaching. One section profiled two sisters, both of whom had suffered from infertility. One had undergone IVF, and the other had been artificially inseminated. I looked at the large, full-color picture of the two smiling sisters with their beautiful children, and I recognized one of them as the woman from class!

In the article, the woman said that she had gone home shaken from a class at her parish where she had learned that artificial insemination was wrong. But she loved her faith and was prepared to defer to the Church. She later discussed all she had learned with her sister, and they both continued to study the issue. Ultimately, they *both* came to see the truth of Church teaching, and both women went to confession. They now educate others on the truth as often as they can.

Witnessing our faith to others in this culture is often uncomfortable to the point of cringe-inducing. Many of us would prefer to crawl into a hole and die rather than speak an unpopular truth to a skeptical or hostile crowd. But if we stay silent, we will never know what good God might have brought about had we spoken. For every ten people who reject what the Church proposes, there may be one who is transformed. And there may be others who initially scoff, but years later put the pieces together.

So, if you ever feel sick to your stomach or embarrassed to share a "hard saying" of our Catholic faith (even to fellow Catholics), please pray and push ahead anyway, speaking the truth in love. God is always ready to honor our feeble efforts!

Keep this in mind when your children begin to ask you about their friends at school who were conceived via immoral means. God will give you the words to speak, and the Church he founded has already given us excellent and reasonable answers to share.

REMEMBER . . .

- The Church opposes fertility treatments that bypass and *replace* the marital act, bringing a third party into conception and turning a child into a manufactured commodity.

- Human beings have a natural and God-given right to come into existence through the marital act of their own mother and father.

- The Church supports fertility treatments that re-pair or heal the body and *assist* the marital act in facilitating conception.

REPRODUCTIVE TECHNOLOGIES

Advice for Little Kids

It's easy to teach little children the natural law by cultivating their desire to find out why things are the way they are. They can learn reasoning skills at a young age and so, when they are later confronted with the distorted nature of technologies like IVF and the disorder they cause, they will easily recognize it.

As you teach your small children how to use their minds to reason, ask them:

- What is this?
- What is it for?
- Where does it go?

Play the Game of "Where Does This Go?"

Reproductive technologies don't come up in conversation or in media as often as the previous issues we've addressed. So, unless your small children have been confronted with the issue, it's best to simply teach them how to see God's design in the world around them. In time, they will recognize when people violate that design.

For example, you can show your child a baby doll and ask how we should take care of it. Make it a silly game! What would you definitely *not* do with the baby? Should we put a baby in the fridge? Or on a table in a storage room? Of course not! That's so silly. Babies should be with their mommies! Even better, use a picture or small model of a ten-week-old unborn baby and ask the same questions.

God designed humans to recognize and embrace truth, so asking if a newly created baby belongs on a table or in the refrigerator instead of the mommy's womb will not likely produce any wrong answers. These fun exercises provide a good foundation for when they get older and will hear about babies—whom we love and want to protect!—being conceived in petri dishes or left in cold storage freezers.

Without even mentioning IVF, you'll help your kids become reflexively protective of all human life and deeply averse to the violence done to unborn children through IVF and abortion (which are fruits of the same tree).

Fun with Polaroid Cameras

Explain to your children that Polaroid cameras (which are popular again!) provide nearly instant photos on film paper that pops out of the camera after taking a picture. When the film first emerges, the picture looks like a brown smudge. But as the image develops before your eyes, the subject becomes increasingly recognizable. Within minutes, the entire image is there, crisp and clear!

Now, imagine you are on a boat on a famous lake in Scotland, and you take a Polaroid picture of the Loch Ness Monster. You excitedly show the Polaroid image to your friend, who takes one look and tosses it overboard, saying,

"Too bad that was just a brown smudge and not the Loch Ness Monster!"[74]

How would you respond to your friend? You would likely be furious and shout, "No! That was a picture of the Loch Ness Monster! You just didn't give it enough time to develop for you to recognize it, and now it's gone forever!"

Likewise, an aborted or destroyed human embryo or fetus was a living human being who had simply not developed into the more "recognizable" stages of life. You could show your child pictures of embryos and tell him that he used to be that small inside of Mommy too, and that that picture is exactly how a person at that stage of development is *supposed* to look.

It's helpful for children to recognize and identify zygotes and embryos because this equips them to object to IVF procedures that treat those littles humans like products. Your children will understand the ontological truth that these are actual children and not "things" that somehow become children later.

Speak to your child about his own time in the womb, perhaps saying, "Ever since you were conceived in my womb, you were so dearly loved by God, by Daddy, and by me!" Or, "From the moment you were conceived—which means 'created'—you were already a boy or a girl, and even your hair color, eye color, and final height had been determined!" My own children marvel when I tell them that they—like all of us!—started out the size of the period at the end of this sentence.

This foundation of how to recognize and treat human beings goes a long way in making the case against the utilitarianism of IVF.

A BRAVE NEW WORLD

For older "little kids," you can use science fiction as a way to comment on the bizarre and evil kinds of science being used today. A good teaching tool is Aldous Huxley's 1931 novel, *Brave New World*.

The main idea is that the world has become a cold, sterile place where natural law has given way to the mindless pursuit of pleasure. In this world, children are grown in laboratories, manufactured and conditioned to fill certain roles in life. The book contains mature subject matter, so it's more of a high school read, but even the first few pages of the book (which are available online) are enough to get kids in upper elementary or middle school thinking about how wrong it is to separate procreation from the marital act.[75]

Explaining IVF

When it's time to explain IVF to tweens, it's best to be more straightforward. A conversation might go like this:

The desire of a husband and wife to have a baby is a very good desire! But when a couple isn't able to have a baby on their own, the way God designed it, they can't just go get a baby any way they want. A child is never, ever "owed" to a couple, or to anyone. The Church tells us that children are a *gift*, and a gift cannot be demanded. God gives us many rights, but a "right to a child" is not one of them.

Firm in the Church's teaching that a child has "the right to be respected as a person from the moment of his conception" (DV 8), you can continue your explanation by saying:

It's so sad that some people believe they are owed a child no matter what, and some become so desperate that they have doctors create a child in a lab—in fact, they create *lots* of children, most of whom end up dying because they are "extras" who are created then thrown out. This is no way to treat human beings! We are to love human beings, not use them! We have to stick with God's plan, or people get hurt, used, and even killed. It's never right to go down that road.[76]

We remind our children that not being able to have children is a great heartache for a married couple, and we must pray for those who resort to desperate measures to get a baby. As your kids become teens, you can explain in more detail about how even a good end can never justify immoral means.

REMEMBER...

- Play games with children to help them learn that babies exist from the moment of conception and that even though we look very different at early stages of our development, we still existed at those early moments of life.

- Remind little children that babies should be kept safe with their parents and not put in freezers, laboratories, or any other place that isn't safe for them.

- Teach older kids that children are a gift, not a right. It is *children* who have a right—to be conceived in an act of marital love and then safely sheltered in their mothers' bodies.

REPRODUCTIVE TECHNOLOGIES

Advice for Big Kids

Once you've laid the foundation for your children about the goodness of natural law and God's created order, your teens will be ready to hear exactly how technologies like IVF hurt men, women, and the children who are created that way. They will be able to see clearly why we must not contradict God's design for marriage and children.

Obliterating Fathers

Long ago, I saw an online discussion among infertile Protestant women who fully accepted IVF. These otherwise good Christian women joked about the pictures one of the husbands took of the "sperm collection" room, which included a large rack of porn magazines, porn on television, and a chair with a pad on it to soak up any spills from the husband's act of masturbation.

The way these Christians laughed and trivialized serious sins like pornography and masturbation hurt my heart. Women who would not normally approve of their husbands masturbating to porn suddenly deemed it moral when its purpose was to "get" a baby. But vice doesn't become a virtue simply because it gives us what we want.

Even if sperm were obtained without masturbation, IVF would reduce husbands to sperm-producing machines instead of lovers who unite with their wives, body and soul, to create a baby from that union. This reduction of men is clearly evident in the case of anonymous "sperm donors" who are only wanted for their sperm. Alana Newman, who was conceived this way, says, "There is an ugly side to our conception: the masturbation, the anonymity, the payment. It's shameful to say, but my father was paid roughly $75 to promise to have nothing to do with me."[77]

When talking about this aspect of IVF with teens, you can bring up the concept of absent or "dead-beat" dads and ask them, "If it's wrong for a dad to walk out on his child, wouldn't it also be wrong never to show up in the first place?" Even when the husband supplies his own sperm for his wife's IVF treatment, there is another question a teen should ponder: should a loving husband, created to protect, subject his wife to the IVF process?

CHILDREN FROM ANONYMOUS SPERM

Alana Newman is the founder of the online support group, anonymousus.org, which acts as a "safe zone" for those affected by third-party reproduction. It brings to light what even secular research is bearing out: the kids of donor sperm are not okay.[3] When the "fertility community" asks why the donor kids are so angry, Newman's own experience and the experience of her donor-conceived peers allows her to answer with confidence: "Because you obliterated our fathers."[78]

Jennifer Roback Morse of the Ruth Institute has called surrogacy, egg donation, and sperm donation "the ultimate forms of parental alienation. One parent separates the child from the other, by design, from conception, for no reason except that they want to."[79] A teen can sense the injustice of robbing a child of his parentage.

Exploiting Women

Your older kids need to understand that, in order to get eggs for an IVF procedure, women have to take a series of drugs that cause *Controlled Ovarian Hyperstimulation*. This forces the woman's body to produce large numbers of eggs so that IVF technicians can harvest them. These drugs can also cause Ovarian Hyperstimulation Syndrome (OHSS), which in its mild form causes abdominal pain, vomiting, and diarrhea. In its severe form it causes blood clots and weight gain of up to forty pounds in five to ten days.[80]

A dear Catholic friend of mine, who was not well-formed in her faith at the time, underwent IVF. After some fifteen rounds of IVF (ultimately using eggs purchased from an anonymous young woman and requiring massive doses of steroids/hormones that induced allergic reactions), miscarriages of multiples, and one near-fatal ruptured ectopic pregnancy, my friend ultimately had a precious son. At least thirty of his siblings did not survive the process, although my friend took great care never to "unthaw" or "selectively reduce" (kill in the womb) any of the embryos. She had each one implanted, even at risk to herself.

The donor egg process (using other women's eggs) carries with it the same parental alienation as donor sperm but is even more exploitative. Seductive $10,000 paychecks are offered to healthy, attractive college-age women in exchange for under-going the grueling and even dangerous process of extracting eggs. You can ask your children, especially your teen daughters, "Is this the way women's bodies are supposed to be treated?"

RENTING OUT WOMBS

Speaking of exploitation, don't forget about the ges-tational surrogacy industry, which Bioethics De-fense Fund attorney Dorinda Bordlee rightly calls "human reproductive trafficking."[81] Like egg "do-nation," it lures women—often vulnerable and low-income—with the promise of big money, then mar-kets them for body parts: we will rent your womb for our use; we will endanger your life and repro-ductive health with the off-label use of drugs; we will manufacture and own the unborn child inside you; and you will agree to the terms of a legal con-tract and cash transaction that benefits the brokers and their profit margins.

If the unborn child is at some point deemed "de-fective" by the purchaser, the surrogate is often ex-pected to "evict the tenant" by having an abortion. She's told, essentially, "You will either destroy the child or face legal penalties and attorney fees that will cripple you financially." It's no wonder that even women who support abortion rights often op-pose this form of human trafficking.[82]

Harming Children

Some teens will still have a hard time with this issue, be-cause they feel bad for infertile couples. They might think it's okay for a husband and wife to endure all of these risks if the result is a happy couple that finally has "a baby of their own." But you should remind your teens that we are often called to sacrifice our will and even suffer ourselves, so that others don't have to suffer.

A married couple's choice to use IVF sends the message that we "have a right" to a child if we think that will make us happy. If that's true for married couples, then why shouldn't single people be allowed to procure themselves a baby if they think that will make them happy? But when we bring children into existence outside the safe boundary of the marital act, we see many nightmare scenarios. Here's just one example:

Chester Moore, an unmarried, fifty-year-old man, hired an egg "donor" to create embryos that were implanted in a forty-seven-year old surrogate named Melissa Cook. When Cook was determined to be carrying triplets, Moore wanted one of the children aborted. Cook refused, saying she would rather adopt the third child. After the children were born, however, Cook's parental rights were severed in accordance with the surrogacy contract she signed. At the time of this writing, the triplets were living in the basement of the house of Moore's elderly parents and had developed severe behavioral issues.[83]

Since the egg "donor" (the biological mother) is anonymous, Cook is the closest thing to a mother these children may ever have. The attorney representing Cook sums up the depressing reality that undergirds IVF and surrogacy: "When the primal bond—as ancient as humankind itself—between mother and child is destroyed, what will be left?"

Even when there are "happy endings," the children are the most expendable part of the multi-*billion* dollar IVF industry. Your teens must be told of the millions of human beings, who, in the earliest stages of their lives, are either destroyed in laboratories when they aren't implanted, kept for years suspended or forgotten in storage freezers, used (and killed) as material for medical research, or "selectively reduced" (aborted) in the womb. Teens who see the wrongness of abortion will easily realize that IVF is not pro-life; it treats human life not as a gift to be cherished but as a commodity to be bought and sold—or disposed of when it is no longer "wanted" or "useful."

Even the child who manages to survive the IVF process is harmed, because he has been created not through the sexual union of his parents, but by hired third parties who have stripped him of his God-given right "to be the fruit of the specific act of the conjugal love of his parents" (CCC 2378). No child should have to know and keep in her psyche that she is the result of her father (often a paid stranger) masturbating into a cup, or that she was the lucky child who missed the IVF doctor's lethal needle that killed her twin, or that she was one of dozens of her siblings who avoided years in the cryogenics freezer.

Once you've carefully and simply explained all of this to your teens, they will see the horror of *manufacturing* babies, whose existence should be brought about only through the loving sexual union of their married parents.

NaPro INSTEAD OF IVF

Unlike IVF and many other assisted reproductive technologies (ART), NaPro Technology is healthy and moral. Developed by Catholics and taught to physicians through the Pope Paul VI Institute in Omaha, NaPro respects women, their bodies, their future children, and God's design. Not only is NaPro much cheaper than IVF, it's far more successful in bringing children to infertile couples. Noted on its website:

"Until 1978, most of the effort in medicine in evaluating and treating women with infertility was placed in trying to identify and treat the underlying causes. In 1978, IVF produced a paradigm shift. It led to a 'skipping over' the causes, and this continues . . . to be the foundational management approach. In essence, this is a symptomatic or band-aid approach to treatment, not one that gets to the root causes . . . . NaPro Technology approach[es] for women who have anovulatory infertility, polycystic ovarian disease, endometriosis, or tubal occlusion, all have statistically significantly higher pregnancy rates than patients with similar conditions treated with in-vitro fertilization."[84]

Overcome Evil with Good

Given the harm, death, and downright creepiness associated with IVF, why do so many people, including some theologians and pastors, condone it? Perhaps it's due to a misguided sense of compassion for those who suffer from infertility, or to a mistaken belief that, because life is always good, it follows that any means used to create life is good. These factors can skew emotions and reason, making the immorality of IVF and other forms of ART one of the most difficult and sensitive things for Catholics to explain.

My friend who underwent IVF hopes that by telling her story other couples will not resort to "barbaric methods," as she calls them, to address the immense suffering of infertility. She and I both want to be clear that her child—who is like a son to me and who is my own son's close friend—is the good that God brought out of these immoral acts.

But just because God can bring good from evil doesn't justify our cooperation with evil. St. Paul rebukes the idea that we may do evil that good may come from it (Rom. 3:8) and says instead, "Do not be overcome by evil, but overcome evil with good" (Rom. 12:21).

Whether conceived morally via the marital act or sinfully via premarital sex, IVF, or even rape and incest, *every child is precious and has the same dignity as every other child.* It is precisely because of the inherent, transcendent worth of every child that we entrust each child's creation to the sacred confines of the marital act and not render him the purchased result of a clinical manufacturing process.

REMEMBER . . .

- We should supplement arguments against illicit reproductive technologies with evidence of how it harms everyone involved.

- IVF, surrogacy, and similar reproductive technologies turn men and women into objects or vendors who disburse their genetic material (their children!) to paying strangers.

- These technologies harm children by *intentionally* creating them to be alienated from their biological parents. They turn babies into commodities, often exposed to contract killing or consigned to cold storage for the rest of their lives.

9

MODESTY

What the Church Teaches

When Trent was visiting the Church of the Holy Sepulchre in Jerusalem, which houses the site of Jesus' tomb, he saw a verbal altercation take place between one of the pilgrims and a priest.[85] He wrote about the incident:

As our group prepared to enter, the Eastern Orthodox priest guarding the tomb was yelling at a woman in our group in a foreign language while holding a piece of fabric.

"What's his problem?" she asked.

I told her, "He wants you to wear the wrap because your skirt is too short."

The priest was not overreacting, because a solemn place like Jesus' tomb (and indeed any public venue) is not the place to flaunt a hemline that is flying "upper thigh high."

The woman still didn't understand, and, struggling to find the words in English, the priest finally blurted out, "*Gesu (Jesus)! Clothes!*"

I'm always saddened when Catholics either don't understand the Church's teaching on modesty or believe that it's a misogynistic way of goading women into covering their "shameful" bodies. But just as chastity is not the same thing as abstinence, modesty is not synonymous with covering up.

If we reduce chastity and modesty to lists of "don't do this" or "don't wear that," then we reduce what was meant to *protect* our dignity and beauty to an arbitrary series of rules that end up *hiding* those things. According to the *Catechism*:

> Modesty protects the intimate center of the person. It means refusing to unveil what should remain hidden. It is ordered to chastity to whose sensitivity it bears witness. It guides how one looks at others and behaves toward them in conformity with the dignity of persons and their solidarity . . . . Modesty is decency. It inspires one's choice of clothing. It keeps silence or reserve where there is evident risk of unhealthy curiosity. It is discreet (2521-2522).

Attitude, Not Just Apparel

When we think of modesty and immodesty today, we instantly think of clothing choices. Although that is part of it, the Church is clear that modesty is also about our *habits of speech and our actions* as well, and it applies to both men and women. However, modesty is not only about what we *project outwardly*, but what we naturally *feel inwardly* when we encounter offenses to it:

> There is a modesty of the feelings as well as of the body. It protests, for example, against the voyeuristic explorations of the human body in certain advertisements, or against the solicitations of certain media

that go too far in the exhibition of intimate things (CCC 2523).

St. Paul likewise exhorts us, "Let no evil talk come out of your mouths, but only such as is good for edifying, as fits the occasion, that it may impart grace to those who hear" (Eph. 4:29).

Intimate things are private rather than public things. Intimacy implies that certain aspects of the body should be displayed safely and exclusively in the marital bedroom, and what happens there should be discussed in a sacred—"set apart"—way. The holy, intimate aspects of our lives should be a joyful mystery and not the subject of some trashy article that promises "Ten Ways to Spice Up Your Sex Life."

The universal point of reference for modesty, therefore, is not merely, "Should I wear this?" but *"Should I reveal this?"*

A modest person radiates self-respect and does not reveal anything in words, actions, or flesh that would offend his dignity as a human being made in God's image. Modest people demand that others see them as persons to be loved, and they do not willfully cooperate with anything that would turn themselves or others into objects for use.

This understanding of modesty helps us answer people in our culture (and even in our Church) who think that almost all discussions of modesty involve inappropriate "shaming."

What a Shame!

The Bible tells us that after God created man and woman, "the man and his wife were both naked, and were not ashamed." But after our first parents sinned, Adam and Eve "knew that they were naked; and they sewed fig leaves together and made themselves aprons" (Gen. 3:7).

What changed after the first sin in human history?

The bodies of Adam and Eve didn't become shameful; their *souls* did. Our first parents were now under the dark power of sin, and they suddenly knew that they could look upon each other with a lustful gaze, communicating the desire to use the other. This corruption of sex, which God gifted to us and wants us to enjoy, led human beings into feelings of shame, especially in the sexual realm.

At the most basic level, shame is an emotion we feel when something that should be private becomes public. This can occur when a personal sin becomes common knowledge; but even non-sinful things can become an opportunity for shame if something we want to be private becomes public—like an embarrassing bathroom accident or a clumsy fall.

When it comes to immodest dress, the feeling of shame is not an indicator that the body being revealed is a bad thing. Instead, it is an interior alarm, signaling that other people are objectifying someone, using that person for selfish gratification. We were made to love people, not use them, and shame protects our dignity by guarding us from acting or dressing in ways that aid others in objectifying us.

DON'T BECOME A SOUVENIR

Pope St. John Paul II said that sexual shame occurs when a person sees that he has become "a potential object of enjoyment for persons of the other sex."[86] A person might feel ashamed after a one-night stand, for example, because the gift of the body, which should remain in the privacy of marriage, now belongs to someone who is not a spouse. The part of that person that is meant for lifelong, faithful love is now just a "souvenir" in the mind of a person who had no moral right to it.

Timeless Wisdom

Being surrounded by and even participating in immodesty of dress, word, and deed can dull our ability to see it and acknowledge its harm. We may try to ignore that the Church and the saints have always considered the virtue of modesty as a pretty big deal, and instead, convince ourselves that our immodest society is just a "corrective" for a too-rigid, outdated mindset. However, if we clear our minds of the secular cultural norms that have formed us over the past decades, we'll notice that all the "tough moral issues" discussed in this book are the result of an initial loss of modesty, the virtue which guards chastity.

In a desensitized culture, things like pornography or homosexuality go from being grave vices that are not appropriate to discuss in mixed company, to off-color jokes, to subjects of casual conversation, and finally ending up as no big deal. But Christians may never jettison a virtue, and we've always had a duty to be modest in word and deed. St. Paul said that "women should adorn themselves modestly and sensibly" (1 Tim. 2:9), and he also warned us to "let no evil talk come out of your mouths" (Eph. 4:29).

YOU'RE CATHOLIC?

A well-known chastity speaker once told Trent that when she was in college, she would make a point to attend daily Mass and not be afraid to share her faith with other students. At the same time, she also thought that there was nothing wrong with provocative dress. She was mortified, then, when she invited a male acquaintance to Mass only to have him say in reply, "Oh, wow. I just never thought you were the kind of girl who goes to church."[87]

> St. Jerome said it well, "Either we must speak as we dress, or dress as we speak. Why do we profess one thing and display another? The tongue talks of chastity, but the whole body reveals impurity."[88]

Catholics today are not used to speaking this way or thinking in these terms. Sometimes we are more embarrassed by talk of modesty than by immodesty itself! But if the witness of the Church and the saints has been consistent for more than twenty centuries, then maybe it's the culture's attitude toward modesty we should suspect, not the Church's.

As we learn to teach our children about the virtue of modesty, let's keep the sentiment of St. Bernard of Clairvaux, a Doctor of the Church, in our hearts: "How beautiful then is modesty and what a gem among virtues it is."[89]

REMEMBER . . .

- Modesty is an attitude that recognizes what is appropriate and inappropriate to reveal and is about thoughts, speech, and deeds as well as dress.

- Modesty of dress does not "cover up bodies that are bad," but refuses to turn the goodness of the human body into an object for exploitation.

- Modesty protects the mystery of sacred, intimate things, which should not be discussed in a casual manner lest they be stripped of their sanctity or profaned.

MODESTY

Advice for Little Kids

"Does anyone know where I can find modest clothes for my daughter?!"

This Facebook plea came from the exasperated mother of a four-year-old, after a long search for decent shorts and skirts. As a veteran mom of eight, I've seen a lot of trends over the past twenty-seven years of parenting, but one trend has unfortunately remained constant: parents lamenting the inadequate selection of fashionable *modest* clothing for young girls.

Another common complaint holding steady or growing? That kids even as young as grade school are using obscene language in public places, loudly and reflexively. These boys and girls seem to have no sense of shame about it, even with many adults and smaller children around, as if they don't believe that such vile language is wrong at all.

We may feel like losing hope, but remember that cultivating modesty in our children is not a lost cause! Let's go over a few simple principles.

For Ladies-in-Waiting

Putting little girls in bikinis and half-shirts may seem adorable when they are in preschool or early grade school, but you're not helping your cause later when you want your tweens and teens to dress modestly. The Church tells us that children in the years of innocence naturally "accept the need for modesty in dress and behavior" (TMHS 79). In other words, at this age you won't be fighting a battle over which clothes are appropriate, so why set yourself up for a battle later?

No need to be extreme or scrupulous, of course. A baby in a diaper on the beach, a toddler whose shirt flies up or whose shorts droop while playing—this is not the same as choosing to dress our little girls in "sexy" styles because it seems cute. If you use your common sense and dress your children like *children*, you can't go wrong.

As girls enter grade school, they'll want more input into their clothing choices, and that is perfectly okay, as long as it's understood that you make the choices *together*. If your daughter wants to start wearing more revealing attire that is trendy among her peers, approach these clothing discussions with a calm confidence.

For example, if your little girl presents you with a too-skimpy outfit as you shop, simply look at it and say, pleasantly, "Oh, that's a really cute pattern, but we need to find something with a little more fabric on it." Or, "I love that color! But let's find something a little more modest. How about this?"

I'm a bit more blunt than most, so my girls might have heard, "Nope, not that one. That shows way too much of your bottom, honey." And then we go along our merry way. Your decision is not a big deal, so don't *make* it a big deal.

I've yet to encounter a little girl who fights back, demanding to expose more of her rear end or midriff. Remember, the latency period is a time of *natural modesty*, so there should be no need to explain the "why" behind the virtue of modesty.

Sometimes a simple, friendly reminder that "we call them 'private parts' because they are private" will reinforce the concept in these early years. Children love and trust their moms and dads, so we don't need to overcomplicate and over-explain.

FOR "LITTLE WOMEN"

When my girls were advancing through the tween years (ages nine to twelve), I remember spending long hours with them at the mall, trying to find shorts that 1) didn't expose the entire leg up to the bottom of the rear end, and 2) were not long, ugly Bermuda shorts that a boy might wear. My girls didn't want their behinds exposed to the world, but they also did not want to look frumpy and weird.

It's worth it to persevere and seek out cute clothes that cover enough skin, even if you have to search every shopping center and online store till you get there. I emphasize *cute* (or, fashionable, classic, fetching) clothes, if you don't want to risk later rebellion. You'll want to avoid fights in the teen years, when peer pressure and the desire to look attractive kicks into high gear, so the time to "normalize" modest but stylish clothing is when they are younger.

For Gentlemen-in-Training

We've seen our culture's desire to strip little girls of their ladylike dignity through clothing that objectifies them. When it comes to boys, it's not generally clothing that debases them, but speech and actions. Our culture strips little boys of their gentlemanly dignity when it teaches them that their natural role in life is to be crude.

Although it's normal for boys to laugh about "poop" and "pee" references when they're little, that should start to fall away as they get older. Personally, my family is pretty "earthy," but if our sons' humor became *more* scatological as they grew, then it might be time to put on the brakes and instruct them that our speech will tell others who we are. Dignity and modesty demand that we don't reduce everything to base potty humor, and this expectation keeps them from progressing into vulgar, sexual humor as they get older.

Notice what often happens when parents who cuss start to have children: they start watching their mouths for the sake of their kids! Assuming normal levels of maturity, even most non-religious parents desire modesty of speech for their little ones, proving a natural-law understanding of modesty, whether or not parents know the virtue by name.

From the time they are young, we tell our boys that "character attracts character." If they want to find good, reliable friends (and one day a virtuous wife), they have to cultivate the habit, early on, of being good, reliable, and honorable. Good and decent people are not going to be attracted to a rude, vulgar, indecent guy.

A MODEST PROPOSAL

I propose getting a bit retro by bringing back the terms *lady* and *gentleman*. Why not? The culture loves all things vintage, so let's revive those beautiful words, which help our children understand their dignity before God and others. "Thank you for acting like a lady and not snapping your gum in my ear!" "Thank you for being such a gentleman by holding the door open for your sister!"

Gentleness, decorum, manners, kindness—all of

these can help us cultivate the virtue of modesty in our young children. As they enter adolescence, you can explain more deeply how modesty ties into authentic love.

Stand Your Ground

Our culture has lost the understanding that some things are meant to be private, and that private does not mean "bad" or "dirty" but rather "intimate" and "sacred." That's why parents must never expose a small child to lewd, crude television shows, movies, video games, or websites. This also includes challenging your child's school administrators when they want to introduce sex-ed curricula (often in a coed setting) that use immodest language and examples that strip the marital act of its private, sacred character.

Some may peg you a prude who shelters your kids too much, but let them talk. A little humiliation never hurt a Christian, and no one said that raising children was easy! Also, no one is suggesting that you isolate your kids from pop culture or society completely, but simply that you protect your children's latency period and confidently form them in the virtues.

By standing firm on these issues, other parents will take courage from your example and be inspired to do the same. There is a communal effect to living modestly and virtuously, because virtue is, quite literally, attractive.

Maybe you're worried about being a hypocrite. Maybe you ask yourself, "How can I tell my kids all this and be an example for others when I sometimes wear immodest clothing or use inappropriate language?"

When I was in college and before my reversion to the Catholic faith, I swore like a sailor and casually used sexually explicit language. These habits can be extremely difficult to break (I still struggle with bad language when I am angry), but kids are smart enough to know that by teaching them well, you are not making excuses for your past (or present) sins and weaknesses.

The key to everything here is this: *do not be intimidated.*

Don't be afraid of "not being liked" by your children, or be cowed into acquiescing when you hear, "But other parents let their kids watch this show (or wear this style)!" When I hear complaints like this from my children, I offer a quick smile or hug and say, "Yes, but God made you *my* child, not *theirs*, and I have a responsibility before God to keep you out of harm's way. I love you so much, and for now you'll just have to trust me on this."

Teaching modesty is easier than it seems, as long as you start early, make it normal, and don't get scared or overreact if or when pushback comes. Building a good relationship with the kids from the beginning (remember, be authoritative and not authoritarian or permissive) is what gives you leverage and keeps your children's hearts attached to yours.

REMEMBER...
- Little girls should practice modesty early so that it's easier to form good habits when they are older.

- Use common sense and encourage girls to wear clothes that make them look like little girls, not "sexy" mini-adults.

- Boys should learn modesty of speech and practice being little gentlemen.

MODESTY

Advice for Big Kids

Every summer for about fifteen years, my parents treated the extended family to a California beach trip. When my two girls were teens, they wore either short swim skirts over their one-piece suits or tankinis with swim shorts—quite a contrast to the other women on the beach. It's not always easy to be the modest ones in a crowd of beautiful, near-naked people, but God sent unexpected encouragement one summer day.

While the girls swam, I was at the hotel pool area with some of our little boys when a gorgeous, tanned young blonde woman approached me. "Are you the mother of the two girls I've seen on the beach who are wearing the one-piece bathing suits?" she asked. I was startled by the question, but I smiled as I braced myself for a bit of mockery or scolding: "Yes, those are my daughters!" I'll never forget her response:

"Well, they are just beautiful in their modest bathing suits, truly striking! It's such a breath of fresh air to see at that age, and I just wanted to thank you and them!"

Thank you, Jesus! It was an awesome consolation.

And it was a nice compliment for the girls to hear, because they've never wanted to look "frumpy." We Miller women aren't glamorous, but we like to be reasonably fashionable and look pretty. We never forced them, but we allowed our teen girls to wear makeup, do their hair and nails, and wear attractive, flattering clothing if they wanted. They never looked like "prairie girls" with shapeless, bland dresses, because we have shown them, through the practice of modesty, how to be *in* the world but not *of* it—how to look lovely without being a slave to our culture's degrading view of women.

"What to Wear" or "Not to Stare"?

Whenever the topic of modesty comes up, countless women (including Catholic women) become indignant and say, "I should be able to wear whatever I want! If someone is bothered by it, that's their problem!" Your daughter may share this misguided "girl power!" opinion and might even repeat a catchy slogan that has found its way into numerous high school newspaper editorials:

"Don't tell us what to wear; teach the boys not to stare!"

But that's a false dilemma. We don't have to choose one or the other. We should teach girls to dress modestly *and* teach boys to respect girls no matter how they dress. Boys shouldn't objectify girls with their eyes and thoughts, and girls should not objectify themselves through their clothing.

Girls should also be compassionate, making it easier for boys and men to have custody of their eyes and minds. Because our hyper-sexualized and gender-confused culture insists that men and women are the same, many women don't understand what immodest dress does to men. We may think men are wired like us, and that although men might *notice* immodest dress, it doesn't take over their minds.

But does it?

In a 2011 study by Princeton psychologist Susan Fiske, a group of men had their brains scanned as they looked at pictures of men and women in varying states of dress. Fiske found that the brain's *premotor cortex* lit up when the men looked at pictures of women in bikinis. This part of the brain is associated with taking action and also lights up when men see images of tools. The research suggests that, almost instinctively, men see immodestly dressed women as some*thing* to act upon and not some*one* to interact with.[90]

Ladies, the truth is that men and women *are* different. That's why, as we will see, porn for men is pictures of sex, and porn for women is words and emotions about sex. Men are visual creatures, and since the Fall they've had to fight both an instinctual desire to see women as objects and a habit of getting arousing images stuck in their heads. It does no good, if we want to foster modesty in our teens, to pretend that these facts are not true.

HELP A BROTHER OUT

Boys must certainly learn self-control, but girls must also recognize the weaknesses men have and help them. St. Paul says that we should "bear one another's burdens" (Gal. 6:2), and that by "sinning against your brethren and wounding their conscience when it is weak, you sin against Christ" (1 Cor. 8:12). Women, who are compassionate and nurturing by nature, should never balk at helping a brother in Christ not to sin. (And those of us with sons truly understand this!)

Boys, Modesty, and Respecting Women

When a boy sees a girl who is immodestly dressed, a good way to overcome temptation is to pray for her. Not just something generic, but praying specifically that no one would use or abuse her, that she would find her vocation, that she not feel harassed and intimidated, and that any man she dates will treat her as a person to be loved, not an object to be used. The more the woman can be humanized in his mind, the less the boy will want to objectify her.

We—and especially fathers out there—must consistently encourage our boys to value women for their true, God-given beauty and dignity. Boys are up for the challenge of being disciplined! If they are motivated, they can keep "custody of the eyes," focus attention on a woman's face, and not give inordinate attention to women who are (often) seeking it through immodest dress. You can also remind teen boys that girls will notice them leering (being that creepy guy who stares), so if they want to have healthy relationships with girls, they must respect them through chaste thoughts and appropriate glances.

Boy should also practice modesty in speech by not talking about women or sexuality in crude ways with their friends. This is not as difficult as it seems. My sons have yet to be mocked or derided for not participating in vulgar or lewd discussions about girls, even at public high schools. In fact, they receive a measure of respect from their peers when they don't join in, and their stance encourages other boys to watch their own words in that area.

Remember how we said that men are made to be heroes? This modeling of virtue for other guys is one way your son can be a "leader" and a "hero" in a battle that every boy knows is not easy. Have him try it and see.

The Language Our Bodies Speak

People who say that modesty is a form of "shaming" don't understand that shame is *good* when it warns us about our own objectification. Nobody, least of all the Church, wants people to feel bad about their bodies. God is the creator and designer of our bodies, which are "fearfully and wonderfully made." Our bodies are very good, but that doesn't mean it's always good to *reveal* our bodies to others.

The immodest woman who says, "Just because I'm wearing this doesn't mean that I want people to look at me sexually!" has bought into our culture's mistaken idea that sex is something external to our identities. According to this view, a person can just proclaim that a skimpy outfit at a party is not trying to elicit a sexual response from men ("I just want to look good and have fun!") but that an equally skimpy piece of lingerie is trying to do just that.

But sexuality isn't something we proclaim to be part of us when we feel the situation calls for it. Sexuality is an essential part of our male or female bodies because we exist as a unity of body and soul. What we do with our bodies matters because, whether we like it or not, the body communicates a language of its own. And since it's wrong to lie with our bodies, this means it is wrong to display body parts in a way that communicates sexual desire when there is no intention to consummate that arousal in the marital act.

WHEN A DRESS SPEAKS VOLUMES

One study followed a modestly dressed woman and an immodestly dressed woman as they chatted in a bar. A man posing as a bar patron asked the men around him what they thought their "chances" were with each of the women.

The study's conclusion will surprise no one. The majority of the men said they would have a better chance of going on a date and having sex with the immodestly dressed woman.[91] Even if a woman

> doesn't mean to, by revealing the mystery of her
> body she is saying that she is a "discount treasure," a
> mystery you don't have to work hard to solve.

Finally, remember our advice to little boys who indulge in crude speech, reminding them that "character attracts character"? The same principle applies to girls. There are ways our daughters can dress that will attract virtuous men and ways that will attract lecherous men.

"But that's not fair! A guy should pursue me based on who I am, not what I wear!"

We must teach our children that sin made the world "unfair," but virtue and living in God's will make this world bearable and even joyful! There is no better gift we give our daughter than to put her on a path to meet a man who also fights for virtue, and who will fight for her no matter the cost.

Mystery, Not Immodesty

Although some girls wear immodest clothes because they like attention from boys, many other girls do so because they just want to be pretty and feel "like a girl." In his book *Wild at Heart*, John Eldredge writes, "Most women feel the pressure to be beautiful from very young, but that is not what I speak of. There is also a deep desire to simply and truly *be the beauty* [emphasis added]."[92] Deep down, women want to be *captivating*, and our girls should captivate everyone's hearts—as did the saints! Modest dress for women isn't just about "keeping boys from sinning." Instead, a thoughtful use of clothing shows the world the transcendent beauty that characterizes our daughters—who are body *and* soul.

There's an unfortunate phrase that is used by some well-intentioned but misguided Christians: "Modest is hottest."

In truth, modesty is not about being "hot" or getting others "hot" in the process. The point of modesty is to understand the goodness of the body and its powerful ability to captivate, arouse, and become "one flesh" with another, ultimately producing life from that marital embrace.

A better slogan might be: *Mystery, not immodesty.*

In the end, every virtue, including modesty, is connected to how God created us and how he wants us to treat others. John Paul II beautifully describes this in his apostolic letter *Mulieris Dignitatem* (*On the Dignity and Vocation of Women*), when he says: "A woman's dignity is closely connected with the love which she receives by the very reason of her femininity; it is likewise connected *with the love which she gives in return*" (30). St. Edith Stein captured a similar insight: "The woman's soul is fashioned as a shelter in which other souls may unfold."[93] Sheltering souls, giving and receiving love—these are incompatible with immodesty, a vice that inherently objectifies. They are incompatible with daring others not to sin just because we want to dress or speak as we please. When our sons and daughters understand that modesty proclaims their God-given dignity, they will find great peace and joy in this much-maligned and misunderstood virtue.

REMEMBER ...

- Teach your children that modesty is not about covering up something that is bad, but about keeping a sacred mystery hidden until it is ready to be revealed in the proper context.

- Boys should not objectify girls in their thoughts, words, and stares, and girls should not objectify themselves through their dress.

- Girls should be mindful of the burden boys have over keeping their minds pure, and boys should pray for girls and respect their dignity by refusing to lust after them.

10

PORNOGRAPHY

What the Church Teaches

When I was little, pornography was something men bought from seedy "adult" shops or from a convenience store's hidden-behind-the-counter stash. It was something boys swiped from an older relative or friend to hide under their mattress.

How times have changed. Today, with the click of a smart phone, hardcore pornography is accessible to anyone, including millions of *children*—many of whom first see it in elementary school.

The scourge of pornography destroys marriages, families, and souls. Porn kills authentic love and has snared even good Catholic men into fierce and seemingly hopeless addiction. But God is more powerful than anything in this universe, so we are not without hope as we remember that, even when it comes to beating pornography, "with God nothing is impossible" (Luke 1:37).

The Perversion of Porn

Tastefully displaying the beauty of the human body in a genuine work of art is not a sin. After all, if you walk through the Vatican Museums or the Sistine Chapel, you can find a fair number of statues and paintings depicting na-ked men and women. What is a sin, however, is displaying the human body in a way that distorts the meaning of sex and invites lustful thoughts. The *Catechism* summarizes the Church's teaching on pornography this way:

> *Pornography* consists in removing real or simulated sex-ual acts from the intimacy of the partners, in order to display them deliberately to third parties. It offends against chastity because it perverts the conjugal act, the intimate giving of spouses to each other. It does grave injury to the dignity of its participants (actors, vendors, the public), since each one becomes an object of base pleasure and illicit profit for others (2354).

In other words, pornography is wrong because of what it does to sex and how it harms those who produce and con-sume it. Pornography "perverts the conjugal act" because it takes what is made to be a sacred, intimate gift of self between husband and wife and turns it into a public performance de-signed on a temporal level to make a profit through addiction, and on a spiritual level to tempt souls to infidelity, shattered families, darkness, despair, and hell itself.

Masturbation and the Meaning of Sex

When I wrote an entire chapter on masturbation in my first book, *Raising Chaste Catholic Men* (RCCM), it was a bit surreal. As I mentioned at the start of that chapter, I had never in my life envisioned that I would be writing extensively on such a subject, and I'm guessing that most folks—at least my Catholic friends and relatives—would not generally choose to read about it!

Because the topic came up in conversations with friends as they asked what I was writing that week, I heard many clever jokes and puns about this particular activity. But whereas most of the jokers were faithful Catholics, a secular friend responded to the topic of masturbation with a simple "Ick." Even non-religious people can sense that there is something deeply wrong with this allegedly normal and healthy behavior. Sex with a partner (even sinful sex) is one thing, but the concept of having "sex" with oneself doesn't even make sense.

Though human beings have a distorted view of sex, deep down there is a subconscious understanding that sex is for uniting people and procreating children. Contraception seeks unity without babies, and IVF seeks babies without unity, but masturbation strips sexual activity of *both* of those purposes. Instead of sex as a self-gift between spouses, masturbation is a solitary act of self-centeredness.

JUST "SCRATCHING AN ITCH"?

Some might argue that masturbation is simply a feel-good release, like having a good sneeze or clearing one's nose and breathing better. But if masturbation is just another way of "scratching an itch," then why do masturbatory acts almost always occur while fantasizing about *another person*? This is just more evidence that sex is made to unite persons, and masturbation perverts this meaning.

The Church on Masturbation

In the Sermon on the Mount, Jesus called God's people to a new standard of holiness. From now on, they wouldn't just be held accountable for their actions—they would also be held accountable for the content and intention of their hearts. He taught, "You have heard that it was said, 'You shall not commit adultery.' But I say to you that everyone who looks at a woman lustfully has already committed adultery with her in his heart" (Matt. 5:27-28).

This makes sense because our actions and choices spring from what we keep in our hearts, be it good or evil. If we grow evil thoughts in our hearts, they will sprout into a weed that chokes our spiritual life and keeps us away from God forever. Jesus goes on to say:

> If your right eye causes you to sin, pluck it out and throw it away; it is better that you lose one of your members than that your whole body be thrown into hell. And if your right hand causes you to sin, cut it off and throw it away; it is better that you lose one of your members than that your whole body go into hell (Matt. 5:29-30).

But should we literally pluck out our eyes or cut off our hands? No. Jesus is using *hyperbole*, a rhetorical device that was common among rabbis of his time, to show that sin is serious and that we must always strive to avoid it. That's why the *Catechism* says of masturbation, "Both the Magisterium of the Church, in the course of a constant tradition, and the moral sense of the faithful have been in no doubt and have firmly maintained that masturbation is an intrinsically and gravely disordered action" (2352).

The Church also teaches that we must have compassion for people, especially youths, whose anxieties and difficulties adjusting to puberty affect their judgment (we will discuss this more in chapter 12). But with God's grace, we parents can lay the groundwork throughout childhood that will protect our little ones from the enemy's snare of pornography, thus preserving their joy and innocence.

REMEMBER...

- The Church teaches that pornography perverts the sacredness of the marital act and harms those who consume it as well as those who produce it.

- Those who use porn and/or masturbate are conditioned to value sex, not as fulfillment of marital vows to another person, but as a selfish way to *use* another person as a means to base sexual pleasure.

- Jesus told us that we'd be accountable not just for sinful sexual behavior, but even sinful thoughts. That's why we must rely on his grace in order to protect our families from sexual sin.

PORNOGRAPHY

Advice for Little Kids

When I was in first grade back in the 1970s, I made the daily trek to my elementary school with a group of neighborhood kids. One day there was a commotion as we passed through a gully; one of the little boys had found a discarded copy of *Playboy* magazine there. I didn't see what was on the pages, but there were whispers about naked women before one of the boys ran off with it.

A few years later, my sister and I were exploring our rented mountain vacation cabin when we came upon a hidden stack of porn magazines. This time there was plenty of time to look. With eyes as wide as saucers and some astonished giggles, my sister and I got our first look at pornography, which we knew was bad and forbidden.

Boy, have things changed for little kids these days.

Kids still stumble upon porn, but now it's hardcore, live action, and everywhere—streaming into every electronic device, even within the sanctuary of the home. Keeping in mind the Church's directive not to disturb the latency period of young children, how do we speak to our little ones about such an insidious adversary as porn?

Back to Basics

The first step to "porn-proofing" your children is helping them understand the sacredness of the body. It's pretty normal for children, and specifically little boys, to explore or play with their private parts. Some boys like their penises more than others, and moms in particular may start to worry that their son is on his way to regular masturbation.

I cannot stress enough that parents who encounter this behavior must not freak out or overreact.

Shaming or alarming a child at this age is counterproductive and may drive him further into this "comforting" habit. A good response is distraction and redirection, keeping your voice calm and pleasant.

If your little guy continues, simply remind him that "we don't play with our private parts," or "that's not a toy, sweetie." Eventually he will understand that, like many other activities (nose-picking, rear-end-scratching), it's just not appropriate or polite to engage in that activity.

KEEPING PRIVATE PARTS PRIVATE

In our home, we've always used the words "private parts," not because we don't use proper names for body parts (we do), but because we like to reinforce the "private" part of the private parts! When children see that their bodies are for public purposes (playing, school, church, visiting friends) and private purposes (bathing, going potty, seeing the doctor with Mommy or Daddy) this will lay the foundation for the practice of modesty and chastity later in life. They will know that their bodies are special and should be treated with special care in different types of settings.

A Thing for Sad People

Younger grade-school-age kids are probably the toughest group to talk to about pornography. They can't easily be redirected like toddlers, and yet explicit talk of sex should not happen this young.

However, since kids are being exposed to this filth at younger and younger ages, we'll need to describe the harms of pornography without sexualizing the discussion. One example of how to approach this subject with young children comes from Catholic speaker and author Matt Fradd.[94] When his seven-year-old son asked, "Dad, what's pornography?" here's how their conversation unfolded:

> "Pornography is pictures that are bad. They're bad pictures that make us want to do bad things and they hurt our brains and our souls."
>
> "Why do people look at it if it's bad?"
>
> "Because it can feel good and exciting. But remember, rats find rat poison good and exciting. And not just rats; if I took some poison pills and covered them in chocolate, and people ate them, they'd probably like them too, wouldn't they?"
>
> "Yeah, but then they'd get sick..."

You can see that our children will understand, but we have to be brave enough to teach them.

Fradd has also described strip clubs and porn shops (which your kids might ask about when you drive by them) as "places where sad people go." This is a brilliant way to condemn pornography and sexual exploitation without turning it into a forbidden fruit. Kids want to be happy, not sad, so we must make the connection with them at an early age that porn will ultimately leave them empty and unfulfilled, not to mention far from Jesus.

I also highly recommend a short book that you can read with your younger children called *Good Pictures, Bad Pictures*, by Kristen Jenson and Gail Poyner. Religious and secular parents alike have found incredible value in this book. It teaches children to identify porn (as opposed to other types of nudity, such as in a science book), why it's demeaning (it "lies" about how people should treat one another), how it will trick your brain into feeling good and wanting more (even as kids feel instinctively sick looking at it, and embarrassed), how the brain can become addicted and be caught in a vicious cycle ("thinking brain" vs. "feeling brain"), and what to do if you see "bad pictures."

THE CAN DO PLAN

Jenson and Poyner recommend the following "CAN DO" steps for your children if they ever stumble across pornography:

- **C**lose my eyes
- **A**lways tell a trusted adult
- **N**ame it when I see it!
- **D**istract myself with something different
- **O**rder my thinking brain to be the boss!

I can't stress enough how helpful this book is. If you want to better understand these steps, pick up a copy.

Finally, let your children know that God doesn't want us to be ashamed of our bodies, and he knows how bad we feel when we misuse the bodies he gave us. Reassure them that you will be there to answer their questions, especially as they work through puberty, and that no matter what happens, you love them. They should always feel comfortable coming to you if they need help with understanding or living out a healthy expression of their God-given sexuality.

REMEMBER...

- Children should be taught early on that their bodies are special and sacred, and that private parts should remain private.

- If the subject of pornography comes up, tell kids there are pictures that people think will make them feel good, but which only end up making them feel sad.

- If a child sees a picture that seems bad, he should put it away and tell you or another grown-up immediately. Assure him that he will not get in trouble.

PORNOGRAPHY

Advice for Big Kids

As I write this, one of my sons is a senior at a large public high school. I recently asked him a question I've asked him before: "Do most of the guys at your school watch porn?" His immediate response was, "Yep. Pretty much every one of them."

If he's exaggerating, it's not by much. Porn use is common at Catholic and charter schools as well, and according to one study sixty-two percent of girls and ninety-three percent of boys are exposed to porn before they turn eighteen.[95] This isn't surprising, as most teens have smartphones and computers that give them 24/7 access.

When children are old enough to hear it, we must sit down with them (especially our boys) and soberly tell them how pornography harms those who use it and those who produce it. Up to this point, you may have only told kids that porn has "bad pictures" that will make them sad. Now it's time to openly expose the rottenness of porn so that it won't become a "forbidden fruit," but something they'll work to avoid at all costs.

"Porn Star" Lies

In his excellent book, *The Porn Myth*, Matt Fradd pulls back
the curtain on the modern porn industry—and his findings
should unsettle your teen's conscience. He must understand
that if he watches porn, he will become an accomplice to the
dehumanization of those who take part in it. For example
(and a warning that this is explicit):

- A 2009 study in the *Journal of Urban Health* said that substance
  abuse and mental health issues are common in the adult film
  industry. It concluded, "Our findings suggest that female
  adult film performers are a vulnerable group that engage in
  and are exposed to many risks to their physical, mental, and
  social health. Although a legal industry, health risks among
  performers are multiple and similar to sex workers in illegal
  industries (for example, street prostitutes)."[96] Another study
  found that porn actors in Los Angeles have higher rates of
  STDs than prostitutes in Nevada.[97]

- In order to meet customer demand for increasingly
  graphic sex scenes, porn actors allow their bodies to be
  brutalized by others. One woman who worked in the
  industry for several years reports, "A female porn star that
  had been in the industry for a while had excessive anal
  intercourse and a piece of her muscle from her anus fell
  out on set while she was filming." Another ex-performer
  describes the horrors she endured: "You get ripped. Your
  insides can come out of you. It's never-ending. You're
  viewed as an object—not as a human with a spirit."[98]

- It's not uncommon for porn producers to engage in human trafficking and sexually assault performers, because
  they're used to treating these women like objects. One

woman says her producer forced her to have sex off-camera and that "prostitution was a form of manipulation producers use to get off and get more scenes out of the women." One former porn actress laments the "ridiculous abuse," observing, "People in the porn industry are numb to real life and are like zombies walking around."[99]

- Most men and women who work in porn do so because they are hoping for easy money or they want to fund a drug addiction (ironically often caused by their work in porn). One study found that porn stars were more likely to both use drugs and to have had sex earlier in life and with more partners than the average woman.[100] Some porn performers call themselves "nymphomaniacs" who can't get enough sex, but usually this is just part of the manufactured fantasy. Even if it were true, though, that doesn't justify abusing them through porn. Just as we don't put people with eating or speaking disorders on display for our amusement, we shouldn't do the same to people who have disordered sexual desires.

You must also tell your son that watching pornography and masturbating hurts him—the Church traditionally refers to masturbation, in line with what the natural law says, as "self-abuse"—and sets him up for failure in his future relationships. Some teens might think they're not at risk because they only look at "soft core" porn like Playboy models or even computer-generated porn that does not contain real people. However, in 2015 a comprehensive survey of different studies concluded that "internet pornography addiction fits into the addiction framework and shares similar basic mechanisms with substance addiction."[101]

GAMBLING WITH YOUR LIFE

Porn addiction is very similar to gambling addiction. Both alter the brain's reward system through visual stimuli, and both cause the user to engage in more extreme behavior in order to experience the same "high." This means that the boy who starts by looking at images of naked women eventually finds that mere pictures alone don't excite him. Over time, he seeks out more explicit, violent, and perverse porn in order to achieve that feeling and level of excitement again.

A Balanced Response

Now, there are two extremes we must avoid when we talk about the sin of masturbation. On the one hand, we should not echo allegedly "enlightened people" (including Christian leaders who should know better) by saying, "It's no big deal," or even, "It's completely natural and healthy!" After all, letting children experiment with pornography and masturbation—and the two are linked—is as foolish as letting them experiment with drugs and alcohol. This is not an exaggeration; pornography re-wires the brain, and the user must seek out more graphic, perverted, and even violent pornography in order to continue to experience a "sexual high."

On the other hand, the *Catechism* says that when it comes to masturbation, "one must take into account the affective immaturity, force of acquired habit, conditions of anxiety or other psychological or social factors that lessen, if not even reduce to a minimum, moral culpability" (2352).

This means that masturbation is subjectively a lesser sin for those, including adolescents, who feel overwhelmed by hormones and anxiety, or whose emotional immaturity prevents them from fully understanding or consenting to this act. This does *not* mean, however, that masturbation and pornography are not serious matters. A teen with anxiety who habitually masturbates will not find maturity, confidence, or social/relational/spiritual health until he leaves this particularly addictive sin behind.

So don't hold back on telling your teen son any of the harsh truths we revealed about porn. You can also mention one more thing he might not expect: porn use will keep him from being a real man who can authentically connect with women and treat them how they deserve to be treated.

Remind your teen about natural law, and how most people know in their gut that masturbation, while common, is not a noble or manly thing. In our sexually corrupted culture, some men may brag about being a "player" who sleeps with many women (and other men may envy them), but I can tell you that when it comes to the "solitary sin," few women and no decent men find compulsive porn use and masturbation truly admirable in a man.

Consider also this advice about masturbation that C.S. Lewis gave in a letter to a young American named Keith Masson. Lewis says one thing that makes masturbation wrong is that it "send[s] the man back into the prison of himself, there to keep a harem of imaginary brides. And this harem, once admitted, works against his ever getting out and really uniting with a real woman." He continues:

> For the harem is always accessible, always subservient, calls for no sacrifices or adjustments, and can be endowed with erotic and psychological attractions which no real woman can rival. Among those shadowy brides he is always adored, always the perfect lover: no

demand is made on his unselfishness, no mortification ever imposed on his vanity.[102]

There is a bit of good news to report: even many non-religious men have become fed up with what porn does to them. They don't want to be "creepy guys" who unconsciously leer at women and make them uncomfortable because they've trained their brains to do that for hours on end in front of a computer. Some men have joined together to create an online support group for those who take up the challenge to stop masturbating (and give up porn, its natural companion).

The group, called "NoFAP" (begun on Reddit), has tens of thousands of members, and, though it is quite specifically not religious or moralistic in nature, it has led to a kind of redemption for those involved. As you can read for yourself on the "Ultimate Benefits" thread, the fruit of living free of masturbation has led these men to wholly unexpected gains, including "more confidence," "better relationships with women," being "more motivated and productive," "better marriages" (for married men), "loss of mental fog," "feeling 'alive,'" and even "clearer skin and deeper voice"![103]

UNHEALTHY NOT TO MASTURBATE?

Your teenager might read in an internet article or hear a teacher in his health class say that frequent masturbation reduces the risk of prostate cancer. The truth is that there are many conflicting studies on this issue, with some saying that the risk of cancer is reduced in men over fifty who masturbate and others saying that masturbation *increases* the risk of developing prostate cancer.[104]

> As of this writing, the American Cancer Society does not list masturbation as even a *potential* factor for reducing cancer risk. But even if it did, masturbation could never be justified. As Jesus said, "It is better that you lose one of your members than that your whole body go into hell" (Matt. 5:30).

What About Girls?

Boys are more likely to struggle with pornography and masturbation, but that doesn't mean you should assume your daughters are immune to these sins. Whereas men tend to be stimulated by visual images of sex, women are often aroused by erotic descriptions of it.

Think of the endless number of trashy paperbacks with muscular, shirtless "Fabio-esque" models on the cover—all marketed to women. *Fifty Shades of Grey*, a poorly written "romance" novel about a woman who becomes a sex slave for a mysterious billionaire, has sold over *120 million copies*—mostly to women! That a woman would write such a book and that women made it a phenomenon shows that females are also greatly enmeshed in and attracted to our porn culture.

You can help your daughter understand how profoundly porn is opposed to her female nature by pointing out the obvious: the R-rated "chick flicks" and sexually explicit novels aimed at women always end with the heroine receiving the lifelong, committed love of one man (even in *Fifty Shades of Grey*). For all the talk of sexual liberation, this shows how women still hope for true and permanent love, never desiring to be used and discarded.

One millennial feminist I know, who has defended the hook-up culture publicly and who backs abortion rights and Planned Parenthood, admits privately that she and her fellow "progressive" feminist friends talk a whole lot about "weddings and babies" in their private conversations. These longings are innate in our feminine nature (even if some women won't admit it out loud), but weddings and babies require a faithful commitment and authentic love that is incompatible with and undermined by pornography of any kind.

Keeping Them Safe

The best way to keep your kids away from porn is to limit their opportunities to be exposed to it. Keep computers with internet access in the family room or another common area. Filtering software can block some inappropriate websites, but many have found it to be fairly useless. Some parents install software like Covenant Eyes that tracks computer usage and lets you know if explicit material is being viewed. I can say with confidence that it's a horrible idea to let younger children have their own laptops, smartphones, or any device that is connected to the internet. Just don't do it. You are the parent, and you can show your child how *not* to give in to peer pressure—by not giving in to it yourself.

As for older kids—remember the son I mentioned at the beginning of this chapter? He had a flip phone through the first three years of high school. Did he love being the only kid without a smartphone? Nope, it was embarrassing. But guess what? Graduating high school without a porn problem is worth it.

The battle against pornography is part of a bigger war for the souls of our children, and our sons are called to be true warrior-heroes. Thankfully, heroes are exactly what God has called them to be. Bred into a man's nature is the desire to fight hard for righteousness. Bishop Thomas Olmsted's exhortation to Catholic men, *Into the Breach*, includes a line that points to our sons' victory against the beast of porn, if we parents help arm them for the battle:

> Imagine standing before the throne of God on judgment day, where the great saints of ages past, who themselves dealt with preeminent sins in their own day, will say to each other, "We dealt with the trouble of lust in our day, but those twenty-first-century men! These happy few battled the beast up close!"[105]

REMEMBER . . .

- Teens can understand that porn is wrong because of the inherent shame associated with what is ultimately a selfish and lonely act.

- Your sons must be taught that pornography harms those who work in the industry, and that if they consume porn, they participate in the victimization of women.

- Porn stunts a boy's ability to become a mature, confident man, and it harms girls by encouraging them to accept a degrading view of sex where they are of little worth to men.

11

TRANSGENDER IDENTITY

What the Church Teaches

A few years ago, I was sitting at the airport waiting to board my flight when I heard some television pundits discussing the North Carolina "bathroom bill." It was so controversial that celebrities and even the NBA threatened to boycott the entire state. The California government went so far as to ban all taxpayer-funded travel there.

And just what was so controversial about the bill, which became law and was then partially repealed under political pressure? It required that citizens use public accommodations that correspond to their biological sex. In other words: women's bathrooms, locker rooms, and showers are for women only, and men's facilities are for men only. The law was passed to prevent situations like this one in Washington State: a biological male who claimed to be a "transgender woman" demanded to walk around—fully nude—in the women's locker room where members of a girls' high school swim team routinely undress.[106]

As I listened to the pundits, my eyes were fixed straight ahead at the airport bathrooms with their usual "Men" and

"Women" signage. What had been an innocuous sight for the previous forty-nine years of my life now felt like a surreal piece of nostalgia. Would my granddaughters remember using bathrooms or locker rooms where males weren't present? Would my younger sons eventually share high school showers with girls who claim they are boys? Would we even be legally *allowed* to have separate, private facilities?

It all felt so bizarre that day, and I wondered how an issue that was non-existent just a year or two before was now, according to powers-that-be, the most important "civil rights" issue of our time.

Understanding Transgender Ideology

In order to grasp this issue and how it affects our children, let's examine two concepts: *sex* and *gender*.

The *sex* of a human being has been and continues to be determined *biologically*. Females have two X chromosomes (XX) from conception and develop female sex organs, whereas males have an X and a Y chromosome (XY) and develop male sex organs. There are cases of "intersex" people (also known as *hermaphrodites*) whose ambiguous genitalia and genetic abnormalities make it difficult to identify their sex. However, the overwhelming majority of people identifying as transgender don't have physical or genetic disorders—a point on which even transgender activists agree—and are clearly one biological sex or the other. (And even in ambiguous cases, we can almost always use science to determine if a human being is male or female.)

So, if sex is about biology and can be determined scientifically, then what is gender?

Until the mid-twentieth century, *gender* was used, not in relation to human beings, but in relation to *words* (i.e., masculine or feminine nouns). However, in the 1960s an infamous psychologist/sexologist named John Money attached the concept of "gender roles" to humans.[107] As a result, *gender* came to refer to one's psychological state, social preferences, and behavior (both sexual and non-sexual). That brings us to today, where the profoundly politicized word "gender" is used by many to describe to how a person subjectively "identifies."

Those who identify as *transgender* claim that their gender—their self-identification as a man or a woman—does not match their biological sex, or what they sometimes refer to as their "assigned sex." A "transgender man" is a biological woman who now identifies as a man. A "transgender woman" is a biological man who now identifies as a woman.

Some people believe they are "gender fluid"—neither strictly male nor strictly female but falling somewhere on a spectrum between those two. In fact, the list of gender identities does not stop at three. In 2014, Facebook unveiled a list of *fifty-eight* "genders" to choose from, including twenty-six versions of being "trans," "gender non-conforming," and "other." After some criticism, they expanded the list to include a free-form field so that people can add their own gender term.

This can be confusing, but a simple way to remember the difference between gender (modern cultural construct) and sex (timeless natural reality) is this: a person's *gender* resides in the mind (subjective/psychological), whereas a person's *sex* resides in the body (objective/biological).

Transgender people who say that their interior identification does not match their biological sex might wear clothes and makeup associated with the opposite sex, take hormones to change their appearance, or even undergo so-called *gender reassignment* surgery (a sex-change operation) so that their bodies more closely resemble their sense of gender identity. Since changing one's sex is impossible, this is really just a surgical mutilation that includes amputating genitalia or building genitalia out of prosthetics or other body parts.

These "treatments" can be shocking, but we must take care not to mock or dehumanize people who have an identity disorder, or what psychologists call "body dysphoria." Those who suffer the feeling of being "trapped in the wrong body" carry a heavy cross. This type of dysphoria, like all others, deserves *appropriate* medical intervention, an empathetic ear, and authentic love.

However, our compassion for those who struggle under such psychological distress should not lead us to go along with a lie, especially as it relates to who we are in God's creation.

Man and Woman He Created Them

As we've already seen, human beings are not "asexual souls." We are not ghosts that have no intrinsic connection to our bodies. Instead, human beings are a true *union* of body and soul. We are incomplete without our bodies, which is why St. Paul noted how unnatural it is to be separated from our bodies at death, and how joyful it will be when our souls are reunited with our resurrected bodies at the end of the world (2 Cor. 5:1-5). Since our body is essential to our human identity, it is not possible for a "female soul" to be trapped in a male body, or vice versa.

In a 2012 address, Pope Benedict XVI criticized the idea that "sex is no longer a given element of nature, [but one that] man has to accept and personally make sense of: it is a social role that we choose for ourselves." He said instead that, "According to the biblical creation account, being created by God as male and female pertains to the essence of the human creature. This duality is an essential aspect of what being human is all about, as ordained by God."[108]

When Jesus spoke with the Pharisees, he made this duality perfectly clear by asking them, "Have you not read that he who made them from the beginning made them male and female?" (Matt. 19:4).

Pope Francis also decried the "indoctrination of gender theory." In a 2016 discussion with the Polish bishops, he denounced "gender theory" as "ideological colonizing" saying: "We are living a moment of annihilation of man as image of God." He asked the bishops to reflect on what Pope Benedict had said to him earlier, that "we are living in an epoch of sin against God the Creator."[109] In 2017, the United States Conference of Catholic Bishops released a letter signed by several other Christian leaders that read, in part:

> The movement today to enforce the false idea—that a man can be or become a woman or vice versa—is deeply troubling. It compels people to either go against reason—that is, to agree with something that is not true—or face ridicule, marginalization, and other forms of retaliation.
>
> We desire the health and happiness of all men, women, and children. Therefore, we call for policies that uphold the truth of a person's sexual identity as male or female, and the privacy and safety of all. We hope for renewed appreciation of the beauty of sexual difference in our culture and for authentic support of those who experience conflict with their God-given sexual identity.[110]

On Being Men and Women

In order to answer those who say the Church is hateful toward those who identify as transgender, we should steer the conversation back to this question: "To what do the words 'man' and 'woman' refer?" Even transgender advocates agree that the terms refer to two objectively different realities. If they didn't, there would be no point in choosing to identify as a woman instead of a man, because they would be the same thing.

So let's ask ourselves, "What do all women have in common that makes them women and not men? Likewise, what do all men have in common that makes them men and not women?"

Although some male celebrities who identify as transgender women like to show off their hair extensions or breast implants, we know that having breasts or long hair is not what makes someone a woman. Both of these things can be lost (through cancer, for example) without a person ceasing to be a woman. Instead, the difference between men and women is found in the design of the created order itself: DNA and sex organs that belong to either the male or female of our species.

Men and women are defined by how they are ordered toward procreating human life. Even if a male or female body cannot procreate through marital intercourse due to infertility, this ordering can still be seen in the very design of the body. A man who cannot gestate a baby is not an "infertile [transgender] woman," he is a male—who was never *made* to gestate. And a woman who gestates a baby, despite having had her breasts surgically removed and using hormones to grow a beard, is not a "man giving birth!" as the headlines scream. She's a woman giving birth, as she was *made* to do, like billions and billions of women who came before her.

If transgender ideology takes full root, the terms *man* and *woman* will lose their meaning. And when this happens, *father* and *mother*—and thus fatherhood and motherhood—will become meaningless as well. There is a drive, already well underway (and quite advanced in some places), to replace *mother* and *father* with the androgynous, generic *parent*,* both socially and in legal documents. With the loss of men and women, we will also lose our understanding of sisters and daughters, brothers and sons. How can we raise well-adjusted men and women who interact with one another in a healthy way, and thus form the foundation of civilization, when no one has any idea what those words mean in the first place? This serious problem is why we must teach our children to uphold the truth about their innate masculinity and femininity, even as they reach out to those who struggle with the truth of who God made them to be.

REMEMBER . . .

- *Sex* refers to observable, biological reality that one is a man or woman. *Gender* refers to the subjective belief that one is a man or woman (an "identity" that resides in the imagination).

- A person's belief or feeling cannot override his or her objective, biological reality.

- Male and female are objective categories God created. Those who are confused about their identity in this area need compassionate help, not further encouragement of a delusion.

---

* California law, for instance, now gives the option to replace *father* and *mother* with *parent* on birth certificates.

TRANSGENDER IDENTITY

Advice for Little Kids

One day, I took some of the younger boys to get haircuts (yes, another lesson at the salon), and the stylist who took the boys' names was clearly attempting to "transition" between the two sexes. This person was friendly and gave a great haircut. We did not say a word of judgment or derision, nor did we exchange glances that might have made this stylist uncomfortable, but simply went about our business as usual.

God Saw His Creation Was "Very Good"

When we got in the car, a discussion ensued. "Was that a boy or a girl?" "I couldn't tell at all!" "The name could've been for a boy or a girl." It can be unsettling not to recognize an adult person's sex, because that identification is so primordial in our psyches. Writer Anthony Esolen once noted that a person's sex is the first thing we notice and the last thing we remember.[111] Think about it: you may not remember the name or hair color of the clerk that helped you at the mall, but you will remember if that person was a man or a woman.

We reinforced to the children that this stylist was a child of God with inherent dignity, and how confused and troubled a person must be to want to change or reject one's very nature. As we do when we encounter anyone in grave confusion or sin (including ourselves!), we reminded the children to pray for that person, and we reiterated what we have taught from the start—and what you must teach: we cannot change objective truth, including the good and right way that God made his world.

I cannot stress enough that parents must form a child in objective truth from the youngest years. We don't get to determine what is true based on our feelings (me, me, me); rather, truth exists outside of ourselves (God's created order), and our job is to seek truth, to find it, and to conform our lives and our wills to it.

Teach your children that God made each of us a boy or a girl—and that's something so beautiful, so *purposeful*, that it's written into our physical being: "From before you were born, and even when you were just a microscopic embryo, science could already tell that you were a boy! God is such a thoughtful, masterful Creator!"

Mr. Mom and Mrs. Dad

When *National Geographic* produced its "Gender Revolution" special issue in 2017, the boy on the cover (proclaimed a "girl") was decked out in pink "girl" clothing and had long, pink hair. The "look" was stereotypical, cultural, superficial, and definitely not inherently representative of the female nature. Just like when Bruce Jenner donned long hair, nails, and a sexy lingerie teddy—stereotypical sex kitten attire—for his 2015 *Vanity Fair* shoot, it seemed more fetish than "female."

What can you tell your children about these displays? Well, if your household is like mine, it's easy to show that "nontraditional" roles and activities and colors and dress have nothing to do with being a boy or a girl.

In our house, for example, Daddy is the main cook. He also cleans, organizes, and occasionally dons pink dress shirts. Mommy often takes the reins when it's time to assemble a cabinet, struggles in high heels, and loves football. These deviations from strict "gender roles" don't change our essence as male or female. Dean is 100 percent man, and I love being a woman!

A young boy desiring painted nails or pink clothes "like a girl," or a grown man donning a teddy, does not change him into a female. My six boys, when little, ranged from "all boy" to "Mom, I need more glitter, and watch me dance!" All of them are boys (or men now), and if they were tempted to think otherwise (as some little boys will be, *especially* given the messed-up cultural cues today), Dean and I gently reminded them, repeatedly if necessary, that they are male.

It's never been a problem to redirect and even be firm at times, which is why it shatters my heart when some parents, in the name of "compassion," *encourage* a delusion in their "feminine" sons or tomboy daughters. Some even seek out doctors to give their children puberty-blocking hormones, which could pave the way to "sex-change" operations later in life.

BE PREPARED

There is a disturbing scenario we have to be ready to confront: parents may be charged with child abuse if they don't consent to a child's "gender" therapy as recommended by health care professionals. A seventeen-year-old in Cincinnati was removed from the custody of her parents because they would not support treatment to make her a "him."[112] Imagine a child telling his teacher or counselor, even at the age of four or five, "I'm not a boy, I'm a girl, but Mommy says that's not true." If a doctor, teacher, or government official tries to intimidate you to accept a "transgender" diagnosis of your child, I recommend contacting a faithful Catholic attorney. And be careful whom you elect to your school boards and legislatures.

Escaping Oneself

We hear more and more cases of parents who help their children "transition," even before the traditional age of reason, and even before the child can tie his own shoes. One famous case involves Thomas Lobel, an eleven-year-old boy who identifies as a girl named Tammy. His adoptive lesbian parents claim that Thomas has identified as a girl ever since he was three, and say they worried about suicide risks if he didn't use hormone blockers to stave off puberty.[113]

There should be protective alarm bells instinctively going off in our brains when we hear any adult say such novel and outrageous things!

These adults ignore the real mental health risks involved in trying to change a child's sex. Johns Hopkins University professor Paul McHugh points to a thirty-year study in transgender-friendly Sweden that found that, ten years after having reassignment surgery, the mortality rate of transgender people was twenty-fold higher than the non-transgender population.[114] (Walt Heyer is one example of sex-change regret, and he has made it his mission to reach out to others who regret their operations, and to educate the public about the harm of such surgeries.[115])

McHugh also noted that in a tracking study of children who "reported transgender feelings" but received no medical intervention, between seventy and eighty percent of them lost those feelings.[116] This debunks the idea that kids who show "gender-nonconforming" traits, or who imagine themselves as being the opposite sex, must be psychologically and medically steered toward being their "transition."

Childhood Fantasies and Fables

Imagine how devastating it would be for a little boy or girl to have a growing, healthy body disrupted with hormones and eventually permanently mutilated (along with mind and spirit) because of the expression of a not-uncommon childish thought. Little kids who are still putting pencils up their noses and can't decide what to have for breakfast should never be given the "freedom" to let a fantasy dictate what biology clearly contradicts. In what other area do we allow tiny children to create their own reality and dictate it to adults?

Also, so what if a young boy is more feminine in his play, fashion sense, or affect? So what if a girl wants short hair, no girly clothes, and likes to eat bugs and fight? None of those things affect the truth of one's maleness or femaleness, as even "progressives" have been saying for decades (but who now seem to have amnesia!).

Many of us know little kids who believe they are cats or dogs—some for a very long time. As one mom said to me, "If we encouraged them to believe they were ponies, they would believe it." The idea that a parent would feed this or any childish whimsy (like claims to be the opposite sex) is ludicrous. I'm with the Church and science on this, and I'd go so far as to say that to mess with a child's mind, body, and spirit by pushing a denial of the child's very nature constitutes child abuse.

Instead of fueling fantasy, let's teach truth through fables. One of the most effective tools for teaching children, one which we must bring back to popular use, is the telling and retelling of classic morality tales. In a world of "transgender" conditioning, I strongly encourage every parent to read and reread "The Emperor's New Clothes" to their little ones, until it is known by heart. Unlike any other, this story uncannily reflects—and exposes as folly—our current acceptance of the "transgender" culture.

In the fable, the whole empire repeats and believes an obvious lie. Even the "smartest" adults, due to the power of suggestion and peer pressure, succumb to the madness. Ultimately, it's a little child who is still innocent and clear-thinking enough to speak the plain-to-see truth.[117] Your children will delight in the story while you inoculate them against the illogical thinking of our day.

REMEMBER...

- We should model a compassionate witness to our children when this issue presents itself.

- Men and women, boys and girls can vary in their preferences and behaviors, but this does not change their objective identity as either a man or a woman.

- Teach your children that there is an objective created reality that God designed and set—for our good. When we let feelings dictate our truth, then our life becomes perpetually confused and unstable.

TRANSGENDER IDENTITY

Advice for Big Kids

At my son's large public high school it is not uncommon to see kids in various states of "gender fluidity," but not simply in the sense of feminine boys and tomboy girls as I saw back in my own public high school in the 1980s. No, these kids are either formally "transitioning" or experimenting with opposite-sex alter egos, both of which have become trendy and faddish.

As parents, we are often lulled by a misguided compassion that keeps us from sharing the truth, even in a loving way. If your compassion (or, let's face it, cowardice) leads you to silence about or sympathy for sin, you are playing into the hands of a truth-denying culture that endangers many souls.

Kids *do not need* wishy-washiness. They need us to graciously, firmly, consistently stand up for the truth.

Remember the words of St. Paul, who hoped that "we may no longer be children, tossed to and fro and carried about with every wind of doctrine, by the cunning of men, by their craftiness in deceitful wiles. Rather, speaking the truth in love, we are to grow up in every way into him who is the head, into Christ" (Eph. 4:14-15). Your gracious *confidence* in these discussions is paramount, so ask the Holy Spirit to give you plenty of it! After all, Jesus said, "Ask and it will be given to you!" (Matt. 7:7).

He Said, She Said?

One source of conflict in your kids' culture might be which pronouns to use for those who identify as transgender. Your teen might be caught up in a discussion about a transgender celebrity, or have a biologically male classmate who now has a female appearance and a new name, and who demands to be addressed with "she" and "her."

These pronoun battles actually present an opportunity for Catholics to turn the tables on critics and point out how they are imposing *their* morality on *us*. After all, it's one thing for a person to claim to be transgender, but quite another to force others to go along with this claim against their will, even requiring them to speak words they don't believe.

If your teen gets cornered on this subject, or even challenges you on it, return to first principles: it's wrong to lie. Additionally, a lie becomes more serious when it is spoken about something significant. This shifts the focus from your child (or you) to the real issue. Here's how this might play out:

Tom: Why do you keep saying [man who claims he's a woman] is a he? That's really hurtful!

Mary: I'm not trying to hurt anyone, but please see where I'm coming from. It's wrong to lie, and if I say [man who claims he's a woman] is a woman, that would make me a liar.

Tom: But it's not a lie! If she says she is a woman then she is a woman.

Mary: Wait, are you saying that merely *saying* or *believing* you're a woman makes you a woman? Why should I believe that? Can a person change his race or his species in the same way?

Tom: Well, it's her own *sense* of self that matters!

Mary: But that still doesn't make it true. There's no evidence, in science or in anything we can measure, that "gender" exists except in the imagination. Morally, I am not allowed to lie for anyone. I hope you can respect that my faith requires me to be honest and speak only what is true.

WHAT'S IN A NAME?

I don't think it's morally problematic to refer to a person by a new, preferred name. Some girls have "male" names and some boys have "female" names. Such things are fluid across times and cultures. But incorrectly using sex-specific pronouns in order to accommodate someone's feelings forces us to lie. Lying is not only a sin, but in this case it denies the way God made a person, so the sin is great.

Identity or Reality?

When a person has a body dysphoria unrelated to sex or "gender," everyone understands that the person needs help. When an anorexic looks in the mirror, she might see someone who is obese, even if she weighs much less than everyone else her age. We don't tell that girl, "That's right, you *are* overweight, and we will help you reach the weight that's right for *you*."

Instead we say, "What you perceive yourself to be, well, that *isn't you*. In reality, you are dangerously underweight, and because we love you, we aren't going to help you harm yourself." That is the loving response.

What about people who think they are a different race or ethnicity? In 2015, the head of the Spokane NAACP, Rachel Dolezal, was discovered to have two white parents. She was forced to resign from her position when some members claimed Dolezal misled them into thinking she was black. Yet Dolezal still maintained that she *is* black, even though her genetics say otherwise. She says, "I feel like the idea of being trans-black would be much more accurate than 'I'm white.' Because you know, I'm not white."[118]

You can see the irony that if Dolezal had claimed she was a black *man*, then her "progressive" critics would have said she was half right. Yet, how can we tell a person she's wrong about her sincere sense of her racial identity, but right about her sense of gender identity—when both exist only in the imagination? There is no logic to saying we *affirm* your "sense" of being a man but we *condemn* your "sense" of being black. Your teens will see the contradiction here.

Surgery or Mutilation?

Another body dysphoria concerns people who identify as being amputees or paraplegics even though they have all their limbs and can walk. Doctors call this Body Integrity Identity Disorder (BIID), but some who have this disorder say instead that they are "trans-abled." Like those who identify as transgender, these people feel disconnected from their own bodies; they seek out doctors to paralyze them or amputate their limbs so that they can be who they "truly are."

One researcher in Canada (who identifies as transgender but not trans-able) explains that the transgender community hasn't supported the trans-able community because the former doesn't want its recent momentum in the court of public opinion to grind to a halt by association with the latter, which almost everyone still understands to be a serious pathology.[119]

Yet if we are rightly disgusted that a doctor would amputate the healthy limbs of a person who suffers from BIID, then why aren't we equally disgusted by doctors amputating the healthy genitals of persons who identify as transgender? This mental gymnastics of holding both positions at once (trans-able = bad; transgender = good) is not tenable, unless we completely obliterate in our own minds that *man* and *woman* mean something objectively, as we know that *healthy* and *disabled* do.

Issues vs. Individuals

The way we talk about issues generally is going to be different from the way we talk to people personally, especially those who are working through these issues. For example, although in a book, article, or on social media I might bluntly describe the horrors of abortion, I'll use different words and tone when speaking directly to a woman who has had an abortion. This does not mean I'm being inconsistent. It just means that we must meet each person where he is and as prudence dictates, while refusing to be silenced from speaking Christ's truth generally.

I wholeheartedly believe, as the Church teaches, that transgender ideology is unreasonable and dangerous; however, my heart breaks for those who are truly confused about their own nature and identity, and who struggle with any kind of body dysphoria or disorder. There is no hatred for these vulnerable people, only outrage that ideologues, activists, and (negligent) health care professionals aid and abet this disordered, tragic way of thinking and living.

Teach your older children that, when they talk with someone who identifies as transgender or loves someone who does, they should spend time listening and asking open-ended questions that allow the person to share his experience. This builds rapport and goodwill, and will give them time to put their own thoughts together when sharing the truth that applies to all. Then, they can discuss our common identity as children of God, and stress that we don't want to lie about people or treat them with disrespect.

Your teen can express to the person that one's "sense of gender" is not what ultimately defines human identity. The goodness and fulfillment of each person can only be found in the God who loves us, created us, and who can even use the trials and sufferings in our lives to make us complete and *truly* happy.

A friend of mine, whom I'll call Josh, began to identify as a girl when he was young, after bullying and his own lack of confidence made him feel unworthy of being a man. He told me:

> I realized I had been trying to fix matters of my heart and soul with transformations to my body. In doing that, I was only further running from facing my history. I had to accept that I was a man, and also learn to understand what it meant to be a man. And through that, I realized it is not the muscles that make the man, but the heart of sacrifice. And I realized that even though I didn't measure up in certain ways, there were no impediments to what I could offer in terms of a heart of sacrifice. Through this, I came to realize that, despite my stature and my lack of "manly" accomplishments, I was indeed man enough.
>
> Why? Because I was created with the ability to sacrifice. And one of the things I realized that I had to sacrifice along my journey to greater self-honesty was my attachment to the idea that I was a girl. For me, that was nothing more than escapism . . . from myself. I just couldn't see it at the time. I have since come to realize that if I were ever to be

dug up after I die, they would find the body of a male. That is my nature. And nature is what nobody can outrun.

When your child's friends have been lied to and gone down dark paths that can never bring true or lasting happiness, when they are weary and broken and at the end of their rope, your well-formed child may be the only one left who has never lied to them. *This* is what we want our children to be for others—imitating Christ in both love and truth—and it's what a confused world needs them to be. As long as they are strong enough in their own interior faith life and in their understanding of natural-law truths, they will be the ones to help pick up the pieces for their friends and others who have been victims of a merciless culture.

REMEMBER . . .

- We should tell those who force transgender ideology that we cannot lie about people, biology, and human nature, and that it is unfair for them to demand that we do.

- People clearly recognize other body dysphoria and identity disorders related to race or disability. We should point out the double standard when those same symptoms in "gender" identity issues are ignored or denied.

- We must be compassionate with those who struggle with their identity, encouraging them to find their true identity in the loving God who created them in his image.

12

HOMOSEXUALITY
What the Church Teaches

When it comes to telling the truth about the sin of homosexual acts, even many Catholics advise that we should not make a big deal out of it because it could "drive people away" and make us seem like "haters." We're told that speaking Christ's truth on this subject amounts to condemnation rather than love.

This is a false dilemma, and so one wonders if perhaps it's not a bit of cowardice, or disbelief in Church teaching, that is behind the admonition to keep quiet on this particular—and very popular—sin.

After all, God never asks us to choose between communicating love and communicating truth. We speak the truth in love (Eph. 4:15). In fact, not doing that with regard to homosexuality is itself a form of "soft" bigotry, because it assumes that people with same-sex attractions are somehow incapable of receiving the truth that God has revealed.

Inclinations vs. Acts

When we talk about homosexuality, we need to distinguish between two things: sexual *attraction* and sexual *behavior*.

Almost everyone has sexual attractions to other people; this is a normal part of our existence as creatures that reproduce sexually. But we all suffer from concupiscence (an inclination to sin), which can override our reason and corrupt our desires, including sexual ones. In his letter to the Romans, Paul describes the struggles and temptations we all face:

> I do not understand my own actions. For I do not do what I want, but I do the very thing I hate . . . . For I delight in the law of God, in my inmost self, but I see in my members another law at war with the law of my mind and making me captive to the law of sin which dwells in my members. Wretched man that I am! Who will deliver me from this body of death? (Rom. 7:15, 22–24).

The Church upholds the truth that disordered desires themselves are not sinful. We cannot control the temptations that spring up involuntarily in our hearts due to original sin, but we *can* control what we do with those temptations and desires and whether or not we act on them. It is those *chosen* actions (including willfully dwelling on sinful desires) for which we will be held accountable. One such desire that is not sinful itself, but that can lead to sin, is sexual attraction to persons of the same sex. According to the *Catechism*:

> The number of men and women who have deep-seated homosexual tendencies is not negligible. This inclination, which is objectively disordered, constitutes for most of them a trial. They must be accepted with respect, compassion, and sensitivity. Every sign of unjust discrimination in their regard should be avoided. These persons are called to fulfill God's will in their lives and, if they are Christians, to unite to the sacrifice

of the Lord's cross the difficulties they may encounter from their condition (2358).

Note carefully that the *Catechism* speaks of *unjust* discrimination. As we saw in our discussion of so-called "same-sex marriage," discrimination simply means to make a selection. When an employer picks the job candidate who has the most experience, he *justly* discriminates (chooses) between the qualified and unqualified applicants. But if he refuses to hire a candidate because the candidate is Irish then he *unjustly* discriminates. Reason tells us that experience and aptitude matter in hiring an employee, but race or ethnicity does not.

When it comes to homosexuality, denying someone basic human rights—to things like food or medical care, for example—because of sexual behavior would represent *unjust* discrimination, to which the Church is opposed. In fact, Mother Teresa's Sisters of Charity operated one of the first homes to care for men who were dying of AIDS.[120] However, not allowing two women to marry one another, or not allowing two men to adopt a child, is *not* unjust discrimination. Why? Because sexual differences and behaviors *do* matter when it comes to the nature of marriage and the task of raising children.

Similarly, when the Church says that people who identify as gay or lesbian "must be accepted with respect, compassion, and sensitivity," that does not mean we must support their sexual behaviors and relationships. It simply means that we are to have the same respect and compassion for them that we would have for any other fellow human being, all of whom struggle with concupiscence and sin.

Unnatural Behavior

When it comes to homosexual behavior itself, the *Catechism* states: "Basing itself on Sacred Scripture, which presents homosexual acts as acts of grave depravity, tradition has always declared that "homosexual acts are intrinsically disordered" (2357). Because sex has always been seen as the means of consummating a marriage between a man and woman, Christians have always considered anything that divorces sex from this life-giving love—be it contraception, masturbation, or homosexual acts—as a grave distortion of our sexuality. The Bible supports this explicitly; for example, Leviticus 18:22 says, "You shall not lie with a male as with a woman; it is an abomination."

When people hear this they often reply, "But Leviticus also says eating shellfish is wrong. Is eating at Red Lobster an 'abomination'?"

Their objection is a clear case of confusing practical, disciplinary laws (which change) with the eternal laws of morality (which do not change). Both kinds of laws are found in the Bible, and the Church identifies and distinguishes between them. For example, the Old Testament also required that roofs have fences, because people often spent time lounging up there (Deut. 22:8). No one thinks that practical rule is supposed to be a universal moral law—but *everyone* accepts that the moral law that prohibits pushing someone off a roof is still binding.

The Old Testament's dietary laws were likewise practical laws that were only meant to keep Jews of that time separate from their pagan neighbors. But Leviticus 18:22 falls in the category of unchanging moral laws, like those banning child sacrifice and bestiality, which appear before and after this verse! Leviticus 18:24 summarizes, "Do not defile yourselves by any of these things, for by all these the nations I am casting out before you defiled themselves." In other words, God punished pagan nations because, though they didn't have the Old Testament or Jewish law, their consciences were created to know and reject obvious wrongs like bestiality, child sacrifice, and homosexual activity.

For people who say, "That's just the Old Testament," they should know that the New Testament reinforces this sexual ethic. St. Paul wrote, "Do not be deceived; neither the immoral, nor idolaters, nor adulterers, nor homosexuals, nor thieves, nor the greedy, nor drunkards, nor revilers, nor robbers will inherit the kingdom of God" (1 Cor. 6:9-10). In this verse, Paul uses two Greek words that refer to people who engage in homosexual *behavior*, and not merely people with these attractions. He is stressing that people who unrepentantly *act* on these attractions will be cut off from the kingdom of God, just like people who let their attractions to money, liquor, or sex lead them to sin.

JESUS "SILENT" ON HOMOSEXUALITY?

Many confused Christians claim that Jesus was silent on the issue of homosexuality and "same-sex marriage." But think: Jesus was also "silent" on child sacrifice, bestiality, and even rape, but that does not *in any way* imply his approval of those things. In truth, the immorality of homosexual acts was so well-understood among the faithful of his time (and for the thousands of years before and after) that he had no need to preach on those subjects.

In his letter to the Romans, Paul describes how Gentiles would be judged for breaking the law God wrote on their hearts. He provides two examples to make his point: idolatry and homosexuality. The idolaters, he explains, "exchanged the truth about God for a lie and worshiped and served the creature rather than the Creator." Those who engaged in

homosexual acts did something similar when "women exchanged natural relations for unnatural, and the men likewise gave up natural relations with women and were con-
sumed with passion for one another" (Rom. 1:26-27).

The apostle's point is that, just as we can know by looking at the created world that it came from a transcendent
God and not some earthly idol, we can also know that
sex is for the union of man and woman just by looking at
the bodies God created for us. The immorality of homosexual acts can be known from reason, by observing the
design of our nature, as well as from divine revelation. As
the *Catechism* says, "[Homosexual acts] are contrary to the
natural law. They close the sexual act to the gift of life.
They do not proceed from a genuine affective and sexual
complementarity. Under no circumstances can they be approved" (2357).

Carrying Our Cross

In this book, we do not use terms like *gay* or *straight* to describe people. Such terminology erroneously reduces one's
identity to one's inclinations, temptations, or desires. This
is a real diminishment, as a person's *true* identity is beloved
child of God, made in his image. Same-sex attractions do
not define people and they definitely aren't something to
celebrate. According to the CDF:

> The human person, made in the image and likeness of
> God, can hardly be adequately described by a reduc-
> tionist reference to his or her sexual orientation . . . .
> [The Church] refuses to consider the person as a "het-
> erosexual" or a "homosexual" and insists that every
> person has a fundamental identity: the creature of God,
> and by grace, his child and heir to eternal life.[121]

The burden of having disordered attractions is like other crosses we humans carry through no fault of our own: things like sickness, temptations to drugs or alcohol, death of a loved one, spousal abandonment, or the need to care for a disabled family member. In these and all cases of trial, our response must be to turn *to* God and *away* from the idea that following a temptation to sin will be easier.

The cross is not incidental to our call to follow Christ but rather an essential part of it. That's why Jesus said, "If any man would come after me, let him deny himself and take up his cross and follow me" (Matt. 16:24). The *Catechism* states that "by the virtues of self-mastery that teach them inner freedom, at times by the support of disinterested friendship, by prayer and sacramental grace, [those with same-sex attractions] can and should gradually and resolutely approach Christian perfection." Daniel Mattson, author of *Why I Don't Call Myself Gay*, writes:

Accepting the truth of our sexual nature honors and defends man's dignity. Humility opens us to discover and find contentment in reality, and live with a daily acknowledgment that we are not our own masters. For me, humility leads me to the truth that I am not my own. It teaches me to be docile to God's will in my life. As Jesus consoles us, "my yoke is easy, and my burden is light" (Matt. 11:30).[122]

REMEMBER . . .

- The Church makes a distinction between attractions (which aren't sinful in themselves) and behaviors (which can be sinful).

- Homosexual behavior is always gravely sinful because it is a distortion of sexuality that contradicts both the natural law and what God has revealed in Scripture.

- People with same-sex attraction should not be reduced to those attractions but given encouragement to carry their cross to holiness and find peace in our Lord.

HOMOSEXUALITY
Advice for Little Kids

When our first three or four children were little, the subject of homosexuality did not dominate the culture. We were still able to follow this advice from the Pontifical Council on the Family: "Homosexuality should not be discussed before adolescence unless a specific serious problem has arisen in a particular situation" (TMHS 125).

You read that right! Parents should not even discuss homosexuality with their younger kids unless there is a serious reason, based on a specific event, to do so.

Fast forward to today.

Dean and I still have pre-adolescent children, but the cultural landscape has drastically changed. The Church's guidance seems almost surreal in a climate where homosexuality is praised in sports, politics, Hollywood, the arts, the medical community, major corporations, and even *children's* television, books, movies, schools, and library story time.

How do we not discuss with our children what our culture unceasingly commands us to celebrate? Even Christian churches (and sadly some Catholic writers and leaders) view "gay pride" as a virtue, and they happily fly the rainbow flag.

Fortunately, there is a second part to that paragraph from *The Truth and Meaning of Human Sexuality* that we can focus on, even if we can no longer shield our little ones from a discussion of homosexuality altogether: "This subject must be presented only in terms of chastity, health and 'the truth about human sexuality in its relationship to the family as taught by the Church.'"

When Your Hand Is Forced

At some point you won't be able to prevent the reality of homosexual behavior from entering your child's life. You may just be walking in the park when your child spots two men or two women holding hands and kissing romantically. Perhaps your child's uncle has a "husband" or maybe an older cousin has "come out."

When this happens, you will have to explain that, although we love our friends and family members who have these feelings, they are confused about God's plan for them. Even at an early age we can teach children that there are ways boys and girls should treat one another (practicing the virtue of chastity) that make sense and should be celebrated, and ways of treating one another that don't make sense and should always be avoided.

Let your child know that romantic love, like the kind mommies and daddies show each other, is only supposed to be between boys and girls. If someone is "romantic" with someone of the same sex, there is a problem, and we can never say that it's good or be happy about it. Still, we love people who are confused about the way God made them, and we pray for them! Stress to your child that we must be kind to every person that God created, but Jesus always asks us to live according to his rules, and that virtuous living will bring us great happiness!

It's good for children to know from an early age that everyone has a cross to carry in life, and some crosses—like the kind where romantic feelings are confused—are very heavy. Some people throw off their cross and give in to temptation and sin, but others choose to imitate Jesus. When we carry our cross just like Jesus did, then we will become saints, joining Jesus in heaven one day, forever!

Parents, if you fear what others might think of you for taking such a stand, remember that what ultimately matters is *not* what other parents or society thinks. What ultimately matters is what God thinks. *You and your spouse are the primary educators of your children, and God will hold you—and no one else—accountable for their formation.*

If we can't withstand mocking or angry comments people might make when we live out our faith, then how will we ever withstand the persecution that Jesus warned us about, which could cost us our livelihoods or even our very lives? (Matt. 10:21-22).

WHEN TO MAKE A SWITCH

In some cases you may have to remove your child from situations that will disturb their innocence. For example, Dean and I recently removed our youngest son from a school that we loved, in part because two of his little classmates have openly lesbian parents. The normalization of this "cool" family structure by other parents made us realize that our little guy needed to be back in a faithful, Catholic school for his formative years. We caused no fuss nor made any grand statements to other parents or school officials; we just quietly made the switch.

The Right Questions

For little ones who should not have to confront the realities of homosexual acts during their latency period, we should take an indirect approach to this issue whenever we can. According to *The Truth and Meaning of Human Sexuality*:

> *Much of the formation in the home is indirect*, incarnated in a loving and tender atmosphere, for it arises from the presence and example of parents whose love is pure and generous. If parents are given confidence in this task of education for love, they will be inspired to overcome the challenges and problems of our times by their own ministry of love (149).

When children see the unique, sacrificial, permanent, and life-giving love that comes from marriage, they will be less likely to embrace the shallow, unfulfilling alternative that our culture offers in its place. But we can't just be good examples. "Sexuality is such an important good that it must be protected by following the order of reason enlightened by faith" (TMHS 55).

Cultivating the *order of reason* in a young child is actually not a daunting task; in fact it can be enjoyable, like a game. Remembering our goal to teach children the natural law by asking, "What is a thing and what is its purpose?" ask your child the following questions:

- Could a boy ever be married to a tree or a car?
- Could a girl ever be married to her pet puppy?
- Why do boys and girls marry each other? (Because they want to become mommies and daddies.)
- Can two boys ever have a baby? Could two girls?

- If being romantic is for mommies and daddies, then could two boys or two girls ever be romantic with each other? Does that make sense?

What If It Were Your Child?

It's hard to believe this next section is being discussed in the "little kids" chapter. However, even elementary school children are "coming out" as gay, transgender, or "fluid" (often influenced by friends, parents, teachers, counselors, or school curricula). So, let's address it.

People sometimes snap at faithful Catholics, "What if *your* child was gay?" This is supposed to expose us either as heartless ideologues who would abandon our children, or as hypocrites who would abandon our principles when it affects our own family. But, as is so often the case, that's a false dilemma.

Of course I would still love my child if he told me he was "gay"! A mother's love for her children knows no bounds, and I will always love my children. The entire vocation of a Christian is to love God and to love others. However, I will not accept my child's sinful sexual *behavior*, just as I would not "accept" my child being a stripper, an adulterer, a corporate raider, or a drug dealer. Sin hurts my child! How could I accept and celebrate *any* sin in a child I love?

"MOM, DAD, I'M GAY."

If your child says this to you, remember our golden rule: *Don't freak out*. As long as he (or she) isn't trying to be a "crusader for a cause," the reason he confided in you is because he's struggling with fear and anxiety, and he knows you are a source of comfort and protection.

In order to be that "firm foundation," give him a huge hug and calmly ask questions like, "How did you come to believe this?" or "What do you think God wants you to do in this situation?" This shows your child that you are committed to understanding him as a person. It also gives you time to assess the situation and respond graciously.

Finally, don't expect to "solve" this issue in one conversation. Take a breath and say a prayer, asking God or the Blessed Mother for the right words in this conversation and many future ones. I also recommend contacting the Courage apostolate that helps people with same-sex attraction live chastely, and their affiliate EnCourage, for parents and friends of those with these attractions.[123]

I will never in a million years condone, confirm, encourage, or celebrate one of my children's sins, but that does not mean I would disavow and hate my child. I would never completely cut off or disown my child if he were living a homosexual lifestyle, but at the same time, I would never betray my Lord by rejecting truth in order to make my child "happy."

Joseph Sciambra, a former gay porn actor who now lives a chaste life, says that when parents cave, supporting and even embracing their children as "gay," those children don't come back to the moral law and a state of grace. Instead, the parents themselves (and often the whole family) end up rejecting the moral law on sexual issues, thus falling away from the Faith. I've seen this happen with families I know. But that's not what God wants us to do when our loved ones turn away from him. Joseph told me, "In the parable of the Prodigal Son, the father—like my own father—did not follow his wayward child. Instead, he wished him well, said goodbye, and proceeded to pray, watch, and wait for his return."[124]

Parents whose child struggles with same-sex attraction should let their child know that they will never stop loving him, because God never stops loving us. Sometimes loving a child means being the only one who will tell him the full truth. Your home and heart will be the one steadfast, faithful place he can come back to after encountering every darkness and dead end.

REMEMBER...

- It's ideal to delay discussing homosexuality until puberty. If this is not possible, talk about the cross people carry when they are confused about their romantic feelings.

- Help your children see that there is a natural order to romantic feelings, rooted in the union that exists between mothers and fathers, husbands and wives.

- Love your child enough to tell him—and hold to—Christ's truth, should he tell you he is "gay."

HOMOSEXUALITY

Advice for Big Kids

In 2017, KLM Royal Dutch Airlines released an ad that went viral on social media, but not for the reasons the company wanted. In an attempt to celebrate Gay Pride Month, the ad displayed three sets of "rainbow" airplane seatbelts: one with male and female ends, one with only female ends, and one with only male ends.

The tagline? "It doesn't matter who you click with."

The irony of this statement was not lost on social media users as they correctly pointed out that it *does matter* if your seatbelt *can't actually click* to restrain you in an accident. As countless jokes flew across cyberspace, it was good to see people having a moment of clarity in the midst of "gay pride" propaganda.

Everyone knows what a seatbelt is for, and where the parts go, just by looking at it. If you misuse it, you can be seriously injured or killed. Likewise, we know what our genitals are for and where "the parts" go just by looking at them. And, as with seatbelts, if people misuse these parts of the body (including through homosexual behavior) grave harm can result.

Both love and reason demand that we not be afraid to defy a wayward culture, and that we use logic to graciously explain why God's design for our sexuality is the one we must embrace.

The Culture of Consent

If your teen or his friends bring up arguments that rely on reasoning like "love is love" or "they're not hurting anyone," you can use an appeal to consequences to show why these slogans, as nice as they sound, don't make sense. You might ask, "If it's okay for adults to have sex as long as they love each other, then what if the two men involved were brothers or the two women were sisters—would that be wrong?"

This is not a purely hypothetical example, because the chaos created by sperm and egg donation has resulted in ever-increasing numbers of people engaging in unwitting romances with half-brothers and half-sisters. But the incest is not always unwitting. The excellent documentary, *Desire of the Everlasting Hills*, profiles three people with same-sex attractions who eventually chose to embrace a chaste lifestyle and return to the Catholic faith.[125] One woman in the film describes what she saw when she and her girlfriend attended a "Womyn's Fest" in the Georgia woods with other self-described lesbians:

> Two women were loving on each other and they turned to face us and I was quite shocked because they were identical twins. I had kind of a visceral reaction. I was really shaken and I said to [my girlfriend], "Are those twins that are making love to each other? Do you think that's right?" And she said, "Well, you know, if we start judging them, then people can start judging us."

Indeed, if "love is love" then why can't *any* consenting adults, including those who are related to each other, have sex? Teenagers should recoil at the suggestion (as we are not yet to the point where incest is widely accepted), and from there, the door should be opened to understanding the principle that sex is not just for expressing affection or feeling pleasure. Reason then helps us conclude that the sexual faculty exists for those who can actually achieve physical union, and which is ordered toward something beyond themselves (procreation). And something that profound and consequential is only appropriate within marriage.[126]

A Natural Conclusion

Recall that natural law is *not* the same thing as "what happens in nature" or "what feels natural for me." This distinction is crucial, because unfortunately many people conflate these ideas. Here are three common, yet confused, objections to natural-law arguments that your teens are bound to hear:

- *Claim: "Homosexuality isn't unnatural because lots of animal species engage in homosexual sex."*

  Fact: In 2004, the *New York Times* reported on two "gay penguins" at the Central Park Zoo named Roy and Silo. The children's book *And Tango Makes Three* describes how the pair incubated an egg and raised the resulting female chick. (It's rarely reported that Silo left Roy in 2008 for a female penguin.)[127] But a behavior is not "natural" for humans just because animals—out of instinct, not reason—engage in it.

  For example, Roy and Silo initially *stole* eggs from other penguins before zookeepers gave them an orphaned egg, but no one would use those facts of "nature" to justify thievery or kidnapping among human beings. You can ask your teen: "Animals naturally steal from one another, force sex on each other, and murder members of their own species. Are those acts, therefore, 'natural' for humans, too?"

Hopefully, your teen will agree that however much *animals* may act that way, it's not natural (and therefore moral) for humans. Sure some humans (like serial killers and rapists) act like animals, but we know that's not the way they *should* act. We humans have rational minds that know right from wrong by examining *human nature* rather than animal behavior.

- *Claim: "If homosexuality is wrong because it is 'unnatural,' then it must be wrong to wear eyeglasses or fly in airplanes! Those don't exist 'naturally' either."*

  Fact: *Natural* in our sense also does not mean "existing in a pristine state untouched by man." Technology like airplanes or eyeglasses are not unnatural, because they do not *contradict*, *oppose*, or (to use a word modern people don't like) *pervert* the natural purpose of the human body. Quite the contrary! Eyes are naturally ordered toward seeing and eyeglasses *restore* that natural purpose. Humans are rationally ordered toward making tools that assist our natural powers of work and locomotion, and airplanes serve those powers. No human society has ever viewed the strengthening and restoration of health, or the development of more efficient modes of transportation, as immoral or contrary to human flourishing. But the man who tries to gouge out his healthy eyes so he can fit in with his blind relatives, or the woman who truly believes she will fly by flapping her arms—these acts can be understood, universally, as going against reason and human nature.

- *Claim: "Homosexuality isn't unnatural, because people don't choose to be gay. They were born that way."*

Fact: We don't know exactly what causes people to have same-sex attraction, but genes are not likely the key. For example, among people with same-sex attraction who have identical twin siblings (with the same exact DNA), it's common for the twin to be attracted to those of the *opposite* sex. But whatever the cause, the belief that same-sex attractions are *innate* (not chosen) does not mean they are *natural*. You could say, "You know, lots of men feel like they want to have sex with more than one woman. It feels very *natural* to them, and they may have felt this way that since puberty. But does that make adultery or polyamory *natural*, or morally right, for humans?" And what of *other* "sexual orientations" besides just "consenting adult, same-sex" or "consenting adult, opposite-sex"? We need not name them all, but are we ready to say that merely *feeling* any particular sexual desire means it's "natural" and something to be explored personally and celebrated publicly?

When we use our minds and examine the human body, we can see what it is *for*. Some humans (those with a disorder called pica) have an innate feeling or desire to eat things like glass, hair, or paint, but that doesn't mean this behavior is *natural* or healthy. The digestive system attached to our mouth and throat only makes sense if eating is designed for food. Likewise, the reproductive systems attached to our genitals only make sense if sex is for the "one-flesh"/procreative union that only a man and a woman can achieve.

"GOD MADE ME THIS WAY"

When people say that "God made me this way," we must not accept that reflexively. God *makes* each person with a profound capacity and desire *to love and be loved*. However, original sin and actual sin distort and derail the good desires that God gave us, as our passions are no longer perfectly under the control of our intellect and will. Explain to your teen that just as a person can struggle for much of his life with a disordered attraction to food, work, money, or alcohol, he may also struggle with a disordered attraction to sex.

God doesn't tempt us to sin, but rather he allows us to endure temptation because his power perfects us in our weakness (2 Cor. 12:9). St. Basil's words may appeal to your teens: "As the pilot of a vessel is tried in a storm; as the wrestler is tried in the ring; the soldier in the battle, and the hero in adversity, so is the Christian tried in temptation."

Right and Wrong vs. Nice and Nasty

The toughest challenges your teen will face are interactions with friends who either have same-sex attraction or know someone who does. Even popular depictions of TV and movie characters who identify as gay or lesbian can reinforce the following idea in your teen's mind: "I like these people and they're gay, so I guess being gay isn't bad after all." This often leads to the belief that only "haters" or "bigots" would say that these nice people are doing things that could doom their immortal souls.

Even if your teen does believe homosexuality is wrong, he may not want to publicly admit it, because that might offend his peers or teachers. That's why we have to remind our children that everyone struggles with sin, including people we truly like.

A kind teacher or coach might struggle with an addiction to pornography or alcohol. A favorite relative may have divorced and abandoned a spouse and children. A dear friend may be addicted to drugs or be abusive with her kids. An action is not right or wrong because a nice or nasty person committed it. Its rightness or wrongness comes from whether it *corresponds to* the natural law (and so it's right) or it *contradicts* the natural law (and so it's wrong).

ANGRY REPLIES TO YOUR GRACIOUS RESPONSE

No matter to whom we are speaking, we should always speak the truth with respect and kindness, knowing that it is individuals who hear us, even if we are speaking to a general audience (this is especially true on social media, where we must keep our decorum). Yet, even if you speak in non-personal, respectful ways, you can expect to be called a hater and worse. This is the nature of an emotional debate, and it's the sort of thing Christ promised that his followers would endure. Jesus himself was the perfect evangelist, but many people called him hateful names, and Scripture calls him the "rock of offense"! (1 Pet. 2:8, ESV).

On social media I have made the case for the immorality of homosexual acts simply by using the words of Christ, the teachings of the Church, and the wisdom of the saints. However, even faithful Catholics will respond by saying, "There's no way I can go up to my gay neighbors and tell them that they are going to hell!"

But no one, and certainly not I, has said that they should do or say such a thing!

Standing up for the truth doesn't mean you have to be nasty or weird; in fact, the most fruitful conversations, and some of the most unlikely friendships, come when both sides understand the distinction between *issues* and *individuals*, what I call the *micro* and the *macro*.

On the macro level, when we speak to many people (for example, on social media), we should give succinct and powerful reasons for why the Church's teachings and the created order are true, good, and beautiful (think of G.K. Chesterton's works or Archbishop Fulton Sheen's homilies). On the micro level (such as personal conversation), we might use different words and tone, presenting the beauty of truth in a slower, more informal way (think of a mother speaking to a beloved child in pain, a friend offering gentle truth in love, or a priest talking mercifully to a sinner in the confessional). Your teens can learn to distinguish the appropriate time and place for each type of interaction.

REMEMBER...

- Use a Socratic-type method of asking teens questions about sexual ethics to help them see that our "culture of consent" doesn't explain basic sexual norms.

- The "unnaturalness" of homosexuality comes from the body's parts being used in a way that perverts, distorts, and contradicts their natural functions, which can be clearly seen when we ask, "What is the nature of a thing?"

- Explain that even kind people can be caught in the snare of grave sin, and so prayer, love, and truth are the answer, not encouraging or affirming them in destructive behavior.

Made to Be . . . Fully Human

By now, my children know the drill.

We might be walking along at the zoo when I see a turtle and ask, "How does a turtle give glory to God?" They humor me, but they know the right answer: "By being a turtle, Mom."

"That's right! A turtle gives glory to God simply by being what he is, what God created him to be! How does a rock give glory to God?"

"By being a rock!"

"Yes, and a tree?"

"By being a tree!"

Every turtle, rock, and tree—in fact, every created thing—gives glory to God by being what it, by nature, is. By being the way it was *made*.

"And a human? How does a human being give glory to God?"

The answer is the same: "By being fully human."

And yet, there is a twist to our nature. Unlike all other earthly creatures, we have the free-will choice to act in accordance with our created nature (virtue) or to act against it (sin). Because we are made in the image and likeness of God with an intellect and a will, we have the freedom to love—or not to love. This is our choice.

Helping our children get to heaven is the primary task given to parents. It is our choice whether to have what can be awkward, tough conversations with them about the issues we discussed in this book. If we choose not to for those reasons, then we are placing our own comfort ahead of our sacred obligation to God and to the souls of the children he put in our charge.

Once we have done our duty to teach and form our children—*God's* children—it's then *their* choice, ultimately, to heed and apply that wisdom to their own lives. If, despite your best efforts, your child has strayed far from the Faith and the moral law, let me offer some words of encouragement.

First, pray without ceasing (1 Thess. 5:17). Offer your sufferings in union with Christ's sufferings, and become a saint (your prayers literally become more powerful as you become more holy!). Abandon yourself to the Father's will and trust that God loves your child even more than you do. You might also ask for the intercession of St. Monica, who prayed for many years before her son, St. Augustine, returned to the Faith.

Second, never despair, but live out your faith in joy and hope! When the world becomes too painful and too dark for your wayward child, he will remember his loving and safe home, and his return to the sure foundation of truth, goodness, and beauty will be a joyous one!

Remember that to be *fully human*—and thus give glory to God—we must embrace our nature. When we know who we are, why we were made, where we are going, and when we act according to our nature and not in opposition to it, *we flourish*. This is true even when life throws overwhelming obstacles in our path.

We humans live, not like a turtle, or a rock, or a tree, but like one who is made to "be like God" (Eph. 4:24), glorified with the Lord, the angels, and saints, forever in heaven.

This book has been a humble attempt to help you teach your children how to understand our human nature, how to act in accordance with the created order, and how to flourish here on earth while awaiting the promise of glory. Friends, let's go forth with joy and confidence into a weary world, giving glory to God in the way only humans can!

A revert to the Catholic faith, **Leila Miller** worked in advertising before becoming a wife and stay-at-home mom. From home, she wrote a regular editorial column for the *Arizona Republic* before starting her blogs, *Little Catholic Bubble* and *LeilaMiller.net*. Leila has been widely featured on Catholic television, radio, and in print, and her books *Primal Loss: The Now-Adult Children of Divorce Speak* and *Raising Chaste Catholic Men* seek to apply the Church's timeless teachings on marriage, family, and the moral education of children. She and her husband Dean have eight children and several grandchildren.

Trent Horn is a staff apologist at Catholic Answers, where he specializes in teaching Catholics to graciously and persuasively engage those who disagree with them. Trent models that approach each week on the radio program *Catholic Answers Live*, where he dialogues with atheists, pro-choice advocates, and other non-Catholic callers. Trent is also an adjunct professor of apologetics at Holy Apostles College and the author of seven books, including *Answering Atheism, Persuasive Pro-Life,* and *Why We're Catholic: Our Reasons for Faith, Hope, and Love.*

Endnotes

1   Dell Elaine Bednar & Terri Fisher, "Peer referencing in adolescent decision making as a function of perceived parenting style," *Adolescence* 38 (2003) 607–21.

2   Thomas refers to the principle multiple times in his writings. For example, "the intellect, according to its own mode, receives under conditions of immateriality and immobility, the species of material and mobile bodies: for the received is in the receiver according to the mode of the receiver," (*Summa Theologiae* I.84.1).

3   Seventh and last joint debate with Steven Douglas, held at Alton, Illinois, Oct. 15, 1858. Cited in Scott Horton, "Lincoln–The Eternal Struggle," *Harper's Magazine*, February 12, 2009, https://harpers.org/blog/2009/02/lincoln-the-eternal-struggle/.

4   Martin Luther King Jr. "Letter from a Birmingham Jail." Available online at: https://www.africa.upenn.edu/Articles_Gen/Letter_Birmingham.html.

5   Saint Thomas Aquinas, *In Duo Praecepta Caritatis et in Decem Legis Praecepta. Prologus: Opuscula Theologica*, II, No. 1129, ed. Taurinen. (1954), 245. Cited in *Veritatis Splendor*, 40.

6   Cardinal Robert Sarah. *God or Nothing: A Conversation on Faith* (San Francisco: Ignatius Press, 2015), 116.

7   Charles Rice, *50 Questions on the Natural Law: What It Is & Why We Need It* (San Francisco: Ignatius Press, 2011), Kindle edition.

8   C.S. Lewis. *Mere Christianity* (New York: Simon and Schuster, 1952), 23.

9   *Summa Theologiae* I–II. 91.2.

10 See J. Budziszewski, *What We Can't Not Know* (San Francisco: Ignatius Press, 2011).

11 Tom W. Smith and Jaesok Son. "Trends in Public Attitudes about Sexual Morality" (2013). Available online at: http://www.norc.org/PDFs/sexmoralfinal_06–21_FINAL.PDF.

12 Jerald G. Bachman, Lloyd D. Johnston, and Patrick M. O'Malley, *Monitoring the Future: Questionnaire Responses from the Nation's High School Seniors, 2000* (Ann Arbor: Michigan, Institute for Social Research, University of Michigan, 2001).

13 Frank Sheed, *Society and Sanity* (San Francisco: Ignatius Press, 2013), 99.

14 Prostitutes were called *porne* and were similar but distinct from the larger class of people who engaged in sexual immorality outside of marriage.

15 Jean M. Twenge, Ryne A. Sherman, and Brooke E. Wells. "Changes in American Adults' Sexual Behavior and Attitudes, 1972–2012," *Archives of Sexual Behavior*, Volume 44, Issue 8, November 2015, 2284.

16 Ibid, 84.

17 I am indebted to Pope St. John Paul II's personalism for this argument from "the language of the body." Similar themes can be found in Alex Pruss, *One Body: An Essay in Christian Sexual Ethics* (Notre Dame, Indiana: University of Notre Dame Press, 2013).

18 Fulton J. Sheen, *Life is Worth Living* (New York: McGraw Hill Book Company, 1954), 61.

19 Kimberly Hahn and Mary Hasson, *Catholic Education: Homeward Bound: A Useful Guide to Catholic Home Schooling* (San Francisco: Ignatius Press, 1996), 214.

20 http://www.usccb.org/news/2015/15–103.cfm.

21 *Considerations Regarding Proposals To Give Legal Recognition To Unions Between Homosexual Persons*, 5.

22 For a thorough defense of this view see Robert George, Sherif Gergis, and Ryan Anderson, *What is Marriage? Man and Woman: A Defense* (New York: Encounter Books, 2012).

23 http://www.catholiclane.com/was-jesus-really-silent-on-same-sex-marriage/.

24 *Considerations Regarding Proposals to Give Legal Recognition to Unions Between Homosexual Persons*, 9.

25 Kristin McCarty, "The Need for a Sociological Perspective on Polyamory," in *Beyond Same-Sex Marriage: Perspectives on Marital Possibilities*, ed. Ronald C. Den Otter (Lanham, Maryland: Rowan and Littlefield, 2016), 148.

26 Steven Erlanger, "At Once Catholic and Secular, France Debates Gay Marriage," *The New York Times*, January 9, 2013.

27 See David Blankenhorn, *The Future of Marriage* (New York: Encounter Books, 2009).

28 Some people will object that our definition means that men and women who are impotent, or cannot physically have sex (as opposed to infertile, which means capable of sex but incapable of conceiving a child) are not capable of marriage. This is a very delicate subject to discuss, precisely because we have forgotten that marriage is a conjugal union. If there is no possibility of a conjugal union, not even one time after marriage, then the essence of marriage is missing. A relationship between two people *without* the ability to have sexual intercourse (i.e., to become "one flesh") is called a friendship. That sounds cold to the modern ear, since we want everyone to feel good and "be happy." But feeling good at the expense of what is true can never satisfy, not ultimately. Impotence or the inability to consummate is an impediment to the sacrament of matrimony for sure, but even the secular state will annul a civil marriage on the basis of non-consummation. Fortunately, with today's technology, there are many ways to cure impotence and allow for marital relations, and that is a blessing.

29 Robert George, Sherif Gergis, and Ryan Anderson, *What is Marriage? Man and Woman: A Defense* (New York: Encounter Books, 2012), 30–31.

30 See "Annulment of Marriage: A Guide" at http://www.paradigmfamilylaw.co.uk/annulment-marriage-guide/.

31 For a thorough review of the consequences to religious liberty that have come from redefining marriage see Ryan Anderson, *Truth Overruled: The Future of Marriage and Religious Freedom* (Washington, DC: Regnery Publishing, 2015).

32 See David Blankenhorn, *The Future of Marriage* (New York: Encounter Books, 2009), xvii.

33 "Homily Of His Eminence Cardinal Joseph Ratzinger, Dean Of The College Of Cardinals," Vatican Basilica, April 18, 2005. http://www.vatican.va/gpII/documents/homily-pro-eligendo-pontifice_20050418_en.html.

34 Leila Miller, *Primal Loss: The Now-Adult Children of Divorce Speak* (Phoenix: LCB Publishing, 2017), 30.

35 See https://www.catholic.com/magazine/online-edition/when-does-the-church-tolerate-divorce.

36 Leila Miller, *Primal Loss: The Now-Adult Children of Divorce Speak* (Phoenix: LCB Publishing, 2017), 30.

37 Available online at https://www.theessentialmother.com/blog-2/what-i-wish-they-would-have-told-me-about-my-parents-divorce.

38 Even the American Bar Association, not known for advocacy of the natural law or

traditional families, addressed the inherent unfairness of no-fault divorce in an article in one of its online journals. The authors propose that no-fault divorce is a "form of [structural] inequality" that puts the children of divorce behind the eight ball compared to their peers with married parents, but is "largely ignored" as such. They propose "'family structure equality' . . . the idea that most children should have the same kind of family structure, one founded on the lifelong marriage of their own married mother and father, also known as natural marriage. This is humanity's anthropological truth, our foundation—preexisting the law of marriage . . . [In] line with overwhelming social science evidence (both past and present), it is the family structure that best ensures equality for children." Jennifer Johnson and Brenda A. Baietto, "Diverse Family Structure: Reevaluating the Best Interests-of-the-Child Standard," *Minority Trial Lawyer*, Vol. 15, No. 4. (Summer 2017), 5.

39   Kristen Harknett, "Why are Children with Married Parents Healthier? The Case of Pediatric Asthma," *Population Research and Policy Review*, Vol. 28, No. 3 (June 2009), 347–365. Kari Hemminki, et al., "Lifestyle and cancer: effect of parental divorce," *European Journal of Cancer Prevention*, Vol. 15, No. 6 (December 2006), 524–530. Vanessa Hemovich and William D. Crano, "Family Structure and Adolescent Drug Use: An Exploration of Single-Parent Families," *Families, Substance Use & Misuse*, Vol. 44, No. 14 (2009), 2099–2113. Robin Fretwell Wilson, "Children at Risk: The Sexual Exploitation of Female Children after Divorce," *Cornell Law Review*, Vol. 86, No. 2, 2000.

40   Howard S. Friedman and Leslie R. Martin, *The Longevity Project: Surprising Discoveries for Health and Long Life from the Landmark Eight-Decade Study* (New York: Hudson Street Press, 2011).

41   Lisa Strohschein, "Parental Divorce and Child Mental Health Trajectories," *Journal of Marriage and Family*, Vol. 67 (2005), 1286–1292. See also Hannes Bohman, et al. "Parental separation in childhood as a risk factor for depression in adulthood: a community-based study of adolescents screened for depression and followed up after 15 years," *BMC Psychiatry*, Vol. 17, No. 117 (2017).

42   Jane Anderson, "The impact of family structure on the health of children: Effects of divorce," *Linacre Quarterly*, Vol. 81, No. 4 (November 2014), 378–387.

43   Bridget Lavelle, "Divorce And Women's Risk Of Health Insurance Loss," *Journal of Health and Social Behavior*, Vol. 53, No. 4 (2012), 413–431. Tahany M. Gadalla, "Gender Differences in Poverty Rates After Marital Dissolution: A Longitudinal Study," *Journal of Divorce & Remarriage*, Vol. 49, Nos. 3–4 (2008), 225–238.

44   Raj Petty et al., "Where is the land of Opportunity? The Geography of Intergenerational Mobility in the United States," *The Quarterly Journal of Economics*, Vol. 129, No. 4 (November 2014), 1553–1623.

45   Nicholas Wolfinger, *Understanding the Divorce Cycle: The Children of Divorce in their Own Marriages* (New York: Cambridge University Press, 2005), 74.

46   Ibid., 113.

47   Peter Kreeft, "Christian anthropology versus the Sexual Revolution," *Catholic Education Resource Center*. Transcript from an address given to The Catholic Medical Association's 79th Annual Educational Conference (October 27–30, 2010).

48   M.K. Gandhi, "Birth Control," *Young India: A Weekly Journal* 7, March 12, 1925, 88.

49   See Angela Franks, *Margaret Sanger's Eugenic Legacy: The Control of Female Fertility* (Jefferson, North Carolina: Macfarland and Co., 2005).

50   See "What is Natural Family Planning," The Couple to Couple League online at https://ccli.org/what-is-nfp/.

51   Gretchen Livingston, "Family Size Among Mothers," *Pew Research Center*, May 7, 2015, http://www.pewsocialtrends.org/2015/05/07/family-size-among-mothers/.

52   The letter has since been reprinted in Uju's book, *Target Africa: Ideological Neocolonialism in the Twenty-First Century*, (San Francisco: Ignatius Press).

53   Cited in Steven Mosher, *Population Control: Real Costs, Illusory Benefits* (New York: Routledge, 2008), 161.

54   https://overpopulationisamyth.com/episode-1-overpopulation-the-making-of-a-myth/.

55   "The world today produces enough grain alone to provide every human being on the planet with thirty-five hundred calories a day. That's enough to make most people fat!" Frances Moore Lappe, Joseph Collins, and Peter Rosset, *World Hunger: Twelve Myths*, 2nd edition (New York: Grove Press, 1998), 8.

56   NaPro refers to Natural Procreative Technology that strives to treat fertility with effective, moral means. See page 151 "NaPro Instead of IVF." See also the website https://www.naprotechnology.com/.

57   https://www.guttmacher.org/news-release/2018/about-half-us-abortion-patients-report-using-contraception-month-they-became.

58   Ibid.

59   Peter Singer, *Practical Ethics*, 3rd edition (New York: Cambridge University Press, 2011), 160.

60   Alberto Giubilini and Francesca Minerva, "After-Birth Abortion: Why Should the Baby Live?", *Journal of Medical Ethics*, 10.1136, 2011.

61   Peter Singer and Helen Kuhse, "On Letting Handicapped Infants Die," in *The Right Thing to Do: Basic Readings in Moral Philosophy*, ed. James Rachels (New York: Random House, 1989), 146.

62   *First Canonical Letter*, canon II.

63   Ronan O'Rahilly and Fabiola Müller, *Human Embryology and Teratology*, 3rd edition (New York: Wiley-Liss, 2001), 8.

64   David Boonin, *A Defense of Abortion* (Cambridge: Cambridge University Press, 2003), 20.

65   Ibid, 99.

66   Jean Garton, *Who Broke the Baby? What the Abortion Slogans Really Mean* (Minneapolis, Minnesota: Bethany House Publishers, 1998), 7.

67   The Congregation for the Doctrine of the Faith teaches that there are "strong grounds for hope that God will save infants when we have not been able to do for them what we would have wished to do, namely, to baptize them into the Faith and life of the Church." From *The Hope Of Salvation for Infants Who Die Without Being Baptized* (2007).

68   See, for example, the videos at the Endowment for Human Development at www.ehd.org.

69   See the website www.secularprolife.org/.

70   Stephen Schwartz, *The Moral Question of Abortion* (Chicago: Loyola University Press, 1990), 15–19.

71   See "Maternal Mortality Rates," The World Fact Book, Central Intelligence Agency, 2010, www.cia.gov/library/publications/the-world-factbook/rankorder/2223rank.html.

72   For a better understanding of the moral difference between direct abortion and procedures that intentionally result in an unborn child's death, see Father Tad Pacholzyk, "When Pregnancy Goes Awry," *Making Sense of Bioethics*, October 2009, https://www.ncbcenter.org/files/9514/6984/9801/MSOB052_When_Pregnancy_Goes_Awry.pdf.

73   The Church teaches that a victim of rape "should be able to defend herself against a potential conception from the sexual assault." This means a victim of rape can use

medicine to prevent *conception* so long as it does not harm a child who has already been conceived. See *Ethical and Religious Directives for Catholic Health Care Services* (Fifth Edition), 36.

74   This comes from Trent Horn and Stephanie Gray and can be found in Trent Horn, *Why We're Catholic: Our Reasons for Faith, Hope and Love* (San Diego: Catholic Answers Press, 2017), 281–283.

75   See "Brave New World," by Aldous Huxley, chap. 1, at https://www.huxley.net/bnw/one.html.

76   Leila Miller, "I Was Astonished to Find this in the Catechism" *Catholic Answers Magazine*, April 18, 2017, https://www.catholic.com/magazine/online-edition/i-was-astonished-to-find-this-in-the-catechism.

77   Alana S. Newman, "Children's Rights, or Rights to Children?," *Public Discourse*, Nov. 10, 2014, http://www.thepublicdiscourse.com/2014/11/13993/.

78   Alana S. Newman, "The Overlooked Fatherless: One Donor-Conceived Woman's Story," IFS, Oct. 26, 2016, https://ifstudies.org/blog/the-overlooked-fatherless-one-donor-conceived-womans-story.

79   Taken from personal correspondence.

80   "Ovarian hyperstimulation syndrome," https://www.mayoclinic.org/diseases-conditions/ovarian-hyperstimulation-syndrome-ohss/symptoms-causes/syc-20354697.

81   Bioethics Defense Fund, BDF Project on Reproductive Trafficking, http://bdfund.org/stories/gestational-surrogacy/ (last visited April 20, 2018).

82   See Kathleen Sloan, *Stop Surrogacy Now: Why We Must Unite*, Public Discourse (May 22, 2015), http://www.thepublicdiscourse.com/2015/05/15037/ and Anna Momligiano, "When Left-Wing Feminists and Conservative Catholics Unite," *The Atlantic*, March 28, 2017, https://www.theatlantic.com/international/archive/2017/03/left-wing-feminists-conservative-catholics-unite/520968/.

83   David Whiting, "Surrogate mom fears for triplets after allegations of abuse by father," Orange County Register, Sept. 23, 2017, https://www.ocregister.com/2017/09/20/surrogate-mom-fears-for-triplets-after-allegations-of-abuse-by-father/.

84   See https://www.naprotechnology.com/infertility.htm.

85   Trent Horn, "Beyoncé! Clothes!", *Catholic Answers Magazine*, Feb. 5, 2013, https://www.catholic.com/magazine/online-edition/beyonce-clothes.

86   Karol Wojtyla, *Love and Responsibility* (San Francisco: Ignatius Press, 1993), 176.

87   This example comes from chastity speaker Melanie Pritchard.

88   *Letter 14.*

89   *Sermon 86*, "On the virtue of modesty."

90   Christine Dell'Amore, "Bikinis Make Men See Women as Objects, Scans Confirm," *National Geographic News*, Feb. 16, 2009, https://news.nationalgeographic.com/news/2009/02/090216-bikinis-women-men-objects.html.

91   N. Guéguen, "The effect of women's suggestive clothing on men's behavior and judgment: a field study," Psychological Reports, 109.2 (October 2011), 635–8.

92   John Eldridge, *Wild at Heart* (Nashville, Tennessee Thomas Nelson, 2001), 17.

93   *Women's Nature and Vocation*, 4. Available online at http://www.kolbefoundation.org/gbookswebsite/studentlibrary/greatestbooks/aaabooks/stein/principleswomeneducation.html.

94   Matt Fradd, "You Need To Talk To Your Kids About Porn," *The Chastity Project*, Jan. 11, 2018, https://chastityproject.com/2018/01/need-talk-kids-porn/.

95   Chiara Sabina, Janis Wolak, and David Finkelhor, "The Nature and Dynamic of Inter-

net Pornography Exposure for Youth," *Cyber Psychology and Behavior* (6), Dec. 11, 2008, 691–693, https://www.ncbi.nlm.nih.gov/pubmed/18771400.

96 Corita Grudzen, et al., "Pathways to Health Risk Exposure in Adult Film Performers," Journal of Urban Health, Vol. 86, No. 1 (January 2009).

97 "L.A. porn stars have more STDs than Nevada prostitutes," *Los Angeles Times*, Oct. 13, 2012, http://latimesblogs.latimes.com/lanow/2012/10/std-rates-in-la-porn-stars-higher-than-in-nevada-prostitutes.html.

98 Matt Fradd, *The Porn Myth* (San Francisco: Ignatius Press, 2017), 68.

99 Ibid, 74.

100 J.D. Griffith, et al., "Pornography actresses: an assessment of the damaged goods hypothesis," *Journal of Sex Research*, Vol. 50, No. 7 (2013), 621–632. Interestingly, the sample of women in this study did not claim to have been victims of child sexual abuse at a rate higher than the average woman.

101 Todd Love, et al., "Neuroscience of Internet Pornography Addiction: A Review and Update," *Behavioral Sciences (Basel)* 5, Sept. 18, 2015, 389.

102 Personal Letter from Lewis to Keith Masson found in *The Collected Letters of C.S. Lewis*, Vol. 3. Cited in Matt Fradd, "C.S. Lewis on Lust, Women, and Masturbation," *Catholic Answers Magazine*, August 13, 2013.

103 See https://www.reddit.com/r/NoFap/.

104 See Daniel J. DeNoon, "Masturbation and Prostate Cancer Risk," *Web MD*, January 27, 2009, https://www.webmd.com/prostate-cancer/news/20090127/masturbation-and-prostate-cancer-risk#1.

105 Thomas Olmsted, "Into the Breach," 18, https://intothebreach.org/wp-content/uploads/2015/10/into-the-breach-roman-catholic-diocese-of-phoenix.pdf.

106 "Transgender woman told to leave women's locker room," October 5, 2012, http://www.kiro7.com/news/transgender-woman-told-to-leave-womens-locker-room/246633184. See also Belinda Luscombe, "Even in Liberal Communities, Transgender Bathroom Laws Worry Parents," *Time*, May 13, 2016, http://time.com/4324687/even-in-liberal-communities-transgender-bathroom-laws-worry-parents/.

107 Keep in mind that Money was also involved in horrific sex reassignment experiments. For more see Phil Gaetano, "David Reimer and John Money Gender Reassignment Controversy: The John/Joan Case," The Embryo Project, November 15, 2017, https://embryo.asu.edu/pages/david-reimer-and-john-money-gender-reassignment-controversy-johnjoan-case.

108 "Address Of His Holiness Benedict XVI On The Occasion Of Christmas Greetings To The Roman Curia," December 21, 2012.

109 Associated Press, "Pope: It's 'terrible' kids taught they can choose gender," *USA Today*, August 2, 2016, https://www.usatoday.com/story/news/world/2016/08/02/pope-francis-children-gender/87956794/.

110 "Created male and female: An Open Letter from Religious Leaders," December 15, 2017, http://www.usccb.org/issues-and-action/marriage-and-family/marriage/promotion-and-defense-of-marriage/upload/Open-Letter-from-Religious-Leaders-Dec-15-2017.pdf.

111 Anthony Esolen, personal conversation with Leila.

112 Kevin Grasha, "Judge paves way for transgender teen to get hormone therapy," The Cincinnati Enquirer, February 16, 2018, https://www.usatoday.com/story/news/nation-now/2018/02/16/judge-paves-way-transgender-teen-get-hormone-therapy/347661002/.

113 Madison Park, "Transgender kids: Painful quest to be who they are," CNN, September 27, 2011, https://www.cnn.com/2011/09/27/health/transgender-kids/index.html.

114 Ibid.

115 See his website sexchangeregret.com.

116 Paul McHugh, "Transgender Surgery Isn't the Solution," The Wall Street Journal, May 13, 2016, https://www.wsj.com/articles/paul-mchugh-transgender-surgery-isnt-the-solution-1402615120.

117 The story is available online here: http://www.andersen.sdu.dk/vaerk/hersholt/TheEmperorsNewClothes_e.html.

118 Mary Bowerman, "Rachel Dolezal, former NAACP leader who claimed to be black, is on food stamps," USA Today, February 27, 2017, https://www.usatoday.com/story/news/nation-now/2017/02/27/rachel-dolezal-former-naacp-leader-who-claimed-white-food-stamps/98469292/.

119 Sarah Boesveld, "Becoming disabled by choice, not chance: 'Transabled' people feel like impostors in their fully working bodies," National Post, June 3, 2015, http://nationalpost.com/news/canada/becoming-disabled-by-choice-not-chance-transabled-people-feel-like-impostors-in-their-fully-working-bodies.

120 Sandra G. Boodman, "Neighbors Are Fearful of Nuns' Caring For the Dying in Convent," The Washington Post, B01, January 12, 1987.

121 "Letter to The Bishops Of The Catholic Church On The Pastoral Care Of Homosexual Persons," 16.

122 Daniel Mattson, Why I Don't Call Myself Gay (San Francisco: Ignatius Press, 2017), 284.

123 See https://couragerc.org/.

124 Joseph Sciambra, personal communication with Leila.

125 The documentary can be viewed online at https://everlastinghills.org/movie/.

126 Incestual sexual union is possible (e.g., brother and sister) whereas two men or two women cannot form a bodily union of any kind. However, incestual marriage is not possible due to the impediments of consanguinity or affinity.

127 According to the senior penguin keeper at the Central Park Zoo, "People read so much into the gay thing, and the gay thing is necessarily a human constraint that's put on top of them." Jonathan Miller, "New Love Breaks Up a 6-Year Relationship at the Zoo," September 24, 2005, http://www.nytimes.com/2005/09/24/nyregion/new-love-breaks-up-a-6year-relationship-at-the-zoo.html.

128 Alexander Jones, "Matthew" in A Catholic Commentary on Holy Scripture, eds. B. Orchard & E. F. Sutcliffe (New York: Thomas Nelson, 1953), 862.

129 Andrew Angel, "God Talk and Men's Talk: Jesus, Tarfon and Ishmael in Dialogue" in Judaism, Jewish Identities and the Gospel Tradition: Essays in Honor of Maurice Casey, ed. James G. Crossley (New York: Routledge, 2010), 107.